GET A LIFE!

CHOKER to non-smoker

CHOKER to

Nicki Defago

Hodder Arnold

A MEMBER OF THE HODDER HEADLINE GROUP

Orders: Please contact Bookpoint Ltd, 130 Milton Park, Abingdon, Oxon OX14 4SB.
Telephone: (44) 01235 827720, Fax: (44) 01235 400454. Lines are open from 9.00 to 17.00, Monday to Saturday, with a 24-hour message answering service. You can also order through our website www.hoddereducation.com

British Library Cataloguing in Publication Data
A catalogue record for this title is available from the British Library.

ISBN-10: 0 340 915404
ISBN-13: 9 780340 915400

First published   2006
Impression number   10 9 8 7 6 5 4 3 2 1
Year   2008   2007   2006

Copyright © 2006 Nicki Defago

Typeset by Pantek Arts Ltd, Maidstone, Kent.
Printed in Great Britain for Hodder Arnold, a division of Hodder Headline,
338 Euston Road, London, NW1 3BH, by Bath Press, Bath.

Hodder Headline's policy is to use papers that are natural, renewable and recyclable products and made from wood grown in sustainable forests. The logging and manufacturing processes are expected to conform to the environmental regulations of the country of origin.

Every effort has been made to trace copyright for material used in this book. The authors and publishers would be happy to make arrangements with any holder of copyright whom it has not been possible to trace successfully by the time of going to press.

CONTENTS

CONTENTS

INTRODUCTION

How many people do you know who smoke? And how many of those people want to give up? The chances are that it will be 100 per cent of them.

My name is Nicki Defago and when I was asked to write *Choker to Non-Smoker*, I thought about all the people I know who have this love/hate relationship with cigarettes. They love them as they sit down in a bar to chat and they inhale the first drag. And by the time they're down to the stub they hate them!

It's very rare to find someone who is genuinely content as a smoker. Now that so much is known about the health risks of cigarettes (not only to smokers but to the people around them), the habit has become so unpopular that even the most thick-skinned person would find it hard not to feel stigmatised. However, if you're someone who genuinely has no desire to stop and feels comfortable smoking – I believe that's a choice that you're entitled to and have no wish to persuade you otherwise.

TOP TIP

- If you are truly in the 'contented smoker' category, you wouldn't have picked up this book – so don't kid yourself!

The *Choker to Non-Smoker* 100-day programme is designed for everyone who, however much they claim to like smoking, knows in their heart that if only they could give up, they would.

The programme is designed to change you from a smoker to a non-choker in 100 days – but of course, you can feel free to speed up or slow down, according to your time and your progress.

Whether you have chosen this book for yourself, or as a present for someone close to you, remember that giving up smoking might be tough, but it's not like climbing a mountain or running a four-minute mile.

The good news is that *everyone* can do it. Good luck!

CHAPTER 1

GETTING READY

Congratulations! Even by picking up this book and reading this far, you've taken a step toward becoming a non-smoker.

Quick quiz

Where do you imagine the most important part of giving up smoking takes place?

a) In the lungs.
b) In the heart.
c) In the mind.
d) In the throat.

The answer is c). Your challenge over the next 100 days is not only to quit cigarettes, but to learn that giving up is not something lost, but something gained. That transformation happens in your head.

Anyone who's given up something they enjoy – maybe they've lost a lot of weight by cutting out cakes and biscuits or gone without butter to lower their cholesterol – knows that it takes time to adjust.

Your notebook

Apart from determination and a real desire to give up smoking, all you need to accompany you throughout the 100-day programme is a notebook. Your notebook will become your companion, where you write down all your thoughts and feelings as you make the transition from choker to non-smoker. Keep your notebook and this book together. Your notebook is important!

◆ Choose one that you like, in bright colours or patterns, to inspire you.
◆ Personalise the cover or get someone to do it for you.

Activity

Get committed!

Psychological research has shown that if you make a written commitment, you are more likely to succeed in making significant changes to the way you live. During the programme you are likely to find some tasks difficult. That's completely normal. You are learning new skills and challenging old beliefs that you've carried around for years, so adjusting will feel strange.

But you'll also feel liberated, as you begin to take control over something that's been controlling you for so long.

Read and sign the following statement:

For the next 100 days, I commit to follow the programme laid down in this book. If I miss a day, or have a relapse, I will not waste time beating myself up and I will not give up. I will do my best to get back on track, with the help of the advice that's offered.

Signature ....

Post a copy of this as your screensaver or stick it somewhere that you look regularly so you're reminded of your determination and your goals. It will help you to stay motivated when the going gets tough.

Every person has a different level of nicotine addiction, which is why some suffer more severe withdrawal symptoms than others. Testing your level will help you to decide whether you'll benefit from additional support (such as Nicotine Replacement Therapy in the form of patches or gum, for example) during the programme.

Activity

How addicted to smoking are you?

1 How soon after waking up in the morning do you smoke your first cigarette?
a) Within five minutes (score 3 points).
b) 5–30 minutes (score 2 points).
c) 31–60 minutes (score 1 point).
d) After 60 minutes (score 0 points).

2 Do you find it difficult not to smoke in areas where it is prohibited – e.g. on a plane or in a library?
a) Yes (score 1 point).
b) No (score 0 points).

3 Which cigarette would you find hardest to miss in the day?
a) The first one in the morning (score 1 point).
b) Any other one (score 2 points).

4 How many cigarettes do you smoke on a normal day?
a) Fewer than ten (score 0 points).
b) 11–20 (score 1 point).
c) 21–30 (score 2 points).
d) More than 30 (score 3 points).

5 Do you smoke more during the first few hours of waking up than during the rest of the day?
a) Yes (score 1 point).
b) No (score 2 points).

6 Do you still smoke if you're ill?
a) Yes (score 1 point).
b) No (score 0 points).

Your score

More than 7 points – Highly nicotine dependent.

4–6 points – Moderately nicotine dependent.

Less than 4 points – Minimally nicotine dependent.

Test adapted from the Fagerstrom Nicotine Dependence Questionnaire.

Don't be put off if you scored highly. There is plenty of help available, which we'll learn about before your Quit Day (the day that you stop – Day 12 in this book). Giving up smoking is about putting you back in control. Knowing how addicted you are to cigarettes will give you the advantage over them!

Self-awareness test

Spend a day noticing how you smoke each of your cigarettes.

- ◆ Do you inhale more deeply at some times than others? If so, when?
- ◆ Do you hold smoke in your lungs for a few seconds or expel it straight away?
- ◆ Do you take a few long, deep puffs, or several 'lighter' puffs on each cigarette?

Make a note of your remarks in your new notebook and check them against the following research, provided by stop-smoking experts.

- ◆ Smokers under stress inhale large volumes of smoke.
- ◆ Bored smokers take more rapid, lighter puffs.
- ◆ Smokers are often unaware of the fact that they adjust the amount of nicotine they put into their system, depending on how they are feeling.

'Knowledge is power.' Sir Francis Bacon

GETTING READY

5

Today you are going to decide on the day you are going to quit. This book suggests Day 12, but *you* are in control and can adapt the day to suit yourself.

The cycle of change

Giving up smoking works on a cycle of change. There are three main stages that take place in a person's mind as they begin to think that they'd like to give up at some point in the future:

1 **Pre-contemplation**. This is when people aren't interested in giving up, but it has been discussed. If you've bought this book, however, you're probably into stage 2 and possibly into stage 3.

2 **Contemplation**. This is the stage when people weigh up what they think the benefits of change will be against what they think the difficulties or disadvantages will be. This stage can be quick for some, or it can take a long time.

3 **Preparation**. People get to this stage when they think the benefits of changing outweigh the difficulties. Now it's time to set a Quit Day, so you get used to the idea that not long from now, you won't be smoking cigarettes.

Take a moment to consider what stage you're at.

I am at stage .... in my preparation to give up smoking.

Activity

Set a Quit Day

Look carefully at your schedule over the next two weeks. Your Quit Day shouldn't be any further ahead than two weeks. This will give you plenty of time to move from stage 2 into stage 3. In this book, Quit Day is set at Day 12.

Sun	Mon	Tues	Weds	Thurs	Fri	Sat

Sun	Mon	Tues	Weds	Thurs	Fri	Sat
				X		

Consider the following points when setting your Quit Day

♦ There will never be a perfect time to give up.
♦ Choose a day that is likely not to be too busy or stressful, and doesn't include a social occasion you've been looking forward to.
♦ When you have chosen your Quit Day, mark it clearly in the grid above, as shown.
♦ Use a bright coloured pen to signify the importance of this day.
♦ Copy the words Quit Day into your daily diary, if you use one, and write the date in your notebook.
♦ Between now and your Quit Day, smoke as usual, but try to be more aware of the implications of smoking.
♦ STICK TO YOUR QUIT DAY.

Be aware!

Notice how often you buy cigarettes. Look at the warning on the packet each time you take out a fag. Try to go without one every so often.

GETTING READY

7

Now that you've set your Quit Day, becoming a non-smoker is becoming a reality. To get used to the build up to your Quit Day, we'll call today Quit Day −8. It's important you feel confident that you will be able to stop. Between now and your chosen Quit Day, we'll prepare both practically and mentally for the adjustment.

The mental shift

How do you feel when you imagine not smoking? In your notebook, write down the first five words you think of in response to this question.

Begin to think of yourself as a non-smoker. If your words include negatives such as 'miserable' or 'stressed', try writing a second column alongside, in which you change the negative word into a positive word. For example:

1 Panic   RELAXED
2 Empty or lost   FREE AND FULFILLED

It doesn't matter if you don't believe what you're writing at this stage. Remember, your mind is set in its ways and it will take time for it to believe the positive benefits you'll enjoy as a non-smoker.

Practical help

Research shows that a combination of methods is the best way to give up for good. Using this book in conjunction with medical intervention will give you the best chance of being a non-smoker for the rest of your life. The following chart shows the percentage of people not smoking after 12 months of giving up, in relation to the method they used.

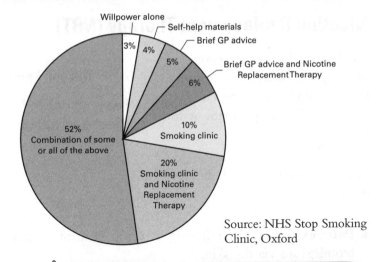

Source: NHS Stop Smoking
Clinic, Oxford

𝒜ctivity

How much do you want it?

- Are you experiencing a physical craving, or is it habit that makes you want a cigarette?
- What could you do to distract yourself if this was after your Quit Day?
- Do you think chewing gum would help? Or phoning a support line (available if you join a smokers' clinic)?
- Begin to think about the type of additional support you'd like to find out about.

Check-in with the doc

Book an appointment with your GP for a few days ahead of your Quit Day. He or she will be able to give you advice on how to stop, and what type of NRT might work best for you. (NRT is explained tomorrow – so don't worry if you haven't come across this phrase before.) Jot down the following notes in your book and take it to your appointment.

- Is there a stop smoking clinic in the area that you could be referred to?
- Is Nicotine Replacement Therapy appropriate for you? If so, ask for details.
- If you have tried to give up many times before, would you benefit from hypnotherapy?

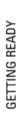

GETTING READY

9

Nicotine Replacement Therapy (NRT)

NRT has helped many people to give up smoking. It's available over the counter at the chemist, or your GP may prescribe it for you.

Did you know?

People who use NRT when giving up are twice as likely to succeed!

NRT comes in several different forms:

◆ **Patches** – work by releasing a steady flow of nicotine into the bloodstream via the skin.
◆ **Gum** – allows you to control your own nicotine dose. The idea is to chew gently, to release the nicotine, which is then absorbed through the lining of your mouth.
◆ **Nasal spray** – the strongest form of NRT. It comes in a small bottle and the nicotine is absorbed very quickly after one sniff.
◆ **Microtab** – a small tablet that sits under the tongue, releasing nicotine through the mouth lining.
◆ **Inhalator** – a plastic device shaped like a cigarette, which allows you to 'smoke', while absorbing a controlled amount of nicotine vapour through the throat lining.

NRT can play an important part in the giving-up process, because (with the possible exception of the inhalator) it helps to keep cravings at bay while you learn to break the habit of smoking. Unwrapping a piece of chewing gum, for example, could replace the routine of taking out a pack of cigarettes and lighting one. Gum and patches are the most helpful forms of NRT, according to some research.

Did you know?

1 piece of gum = $^1/_3$ of a cigarette. Although NRT feeds your body with nicotine while you learn to adapt to not smoking, it's not nearly as bad for you as a cigarette. You won't be taking in the toxins and chemicals contained in a cigarette – only the nicotine, which is the addictive component.

Health hazard

◆ Don't start using NRT until your Quit Day.
◆ It is not designed to be taken while you continue to smoke.
◆ You must not smoke and take NRT at the same time.

Activity
Get extra support

If you can use the internet, take a few moments to look up additional methods that might help you throughout the 100-day programme. Use the search words 'no smoking methods' or 'giving up cigarettes' to get you started. Throughout the programme you'll need to watch out for negative thoughts that try to over-ride your willpower and sabotage your progress. Write down any tips or suggestions that appeal to you in your notebook for easy reference.

TOP TIP

● Think of the 100-day programme as a gradual process of change.
● Think of creating a whole new you!

GETTING READY

11

It doesn't really matter how you give up smoking – as long as you do give up!

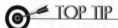 **TOP TIP**

- Puzzles, crosswords and quizzes are all good means of distraction when you crave a cigarette. Cravings can be intense, but they only last for a couple of minutes at a time. Poring over a puzzle will outlast a craving.

The best method for you

If this is your first or second attempt to give up, NRT should give you a real boost in addition to your own willpower. But if you feel you want extra support, help is at hand. Giving up smoking is personal to you – so you must select the method that appeals to you most.

Hypnotherapy

When a patient is hypnotised they experience a sense of deep relaxation. In this state, he or she is very receptive to suggestions made by the therapist. Ask in the library, quiz your GP or do an internet search to find out more.

Acupuncture

The British Acupuncture Council advises that although treatment can help with withdrawal symptoms, it won't cure the habitual aspect of smoking. Treatment involves inserting very fine needles into the ear – the same points are used for all types of drug addiction. This area influences the nervous system, calms the mind and helps the body detoxify.

Smoking clinics

The NHS runs smoking clinics and there are plenty of private services available too. Usually, you'll be offered one-hour weekly appointments for about six weeks. If you stop smoking you can continue receiving help and support for up to a year by attending monthly groups for ex-smokers.

GETTING READY

12

When you book treatments of any kind, ask the therapist to show you his or her professional credentials. It's best to get a recommendation from someone who has been to the practice and was pleased with the service.

These types of additional support do cost money. But remember that, in the long run, paying for treatment that helps you give up will be far cheaper than a lifetime buying fags!

Did you know?

You must chew nicotine gum slowly, then rest, for it to reach its maximum effect. When you feel a strong taste in your mouth, stop chewing and 'store' the gum at the side of your mouth. If you keep chewing, too much nicotine will be released into your system for it to work properly.

Activity

Which support method?

Now that you've looked at the possible support options available to you, make a decision as to which method you are going to go with and stick with it. Tick off the following points in the run up to your Quit Day:

● Ask a chemist about types of NRT.

● Buy stocks of NRT.

● Read any information leaflets properly ahead of your Quit Day.

● Plan distraction techniques to boost your willpower.

● Research/make an appointment with an acupuncture or hypnotherapy clinic.

GETTING READY

Look what you're putting into your system every time you inhale! Spend a few moments thinking about what's in a cigarette.

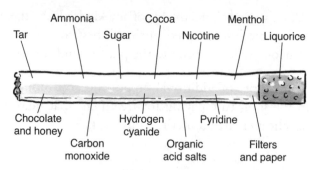

In addition to the contents shown on the diagram, every cigarette contains lots of chemicals that you'd never think of putting into your body in normal circumstances.

Poison	Common uses
Acetone	Nail varnish remover
Acetic acid	Vinegar
Ammonia	Cleaning agent
Arsenic	Ant poison in the USA
Benzene	Petrol fumes
Carbon monoxide	Exhaust fumes
Carbon tetrachloride	Dry cleaning fluid
DDT	Insecticide
Formaldehyde	Embalming fluid
Hydrogen cyanide	Industrial pollutant
Hydrogen sulphide	Stink bombs
Lead	Batteries, petrol fumes
Methanol	Rocket fuel
Nicotine	Insecticide
Polonium-210	Radioactive fallout
Radon	Radioactive gas
Sulphuric acid	Power station emissions
Tars	Road surface tar
Caesium	Heavy metal
Ethanol	Anti-freeze

GETTING READY

Did you know?

Entertainer Roy Castle died of lung cancer in 1994 when he was 62, even though he never smoked. He devoted the last few months of his life urging people to quit and raising awareness about the dangers of passive smoking. 'Whilst playing the trumpet in smoky rooms I inhaled great gulps of air because you have to fill your lungs,' he explained shortly before he died.

Activity

A chemical cocktail

● Take a look through your kitchen cupboard and bathroom cabinet.

● Select a few bottles and line them up on a flat surface. Perhaps you've chosen nail varnish remover, de-icer and cleaning fluid?

● Now, look at the table of chemicals again. Could you imagine eating or drinking this stuff?

Every time you smoke a cigarette, you are putting some of the contents of these bottles into your body.

As well as practical tools like NRT, it's important to learn about the psychological reasons that you smoke.

Tick list

Could you put yourself in any of the following categories? Tick the phrases that apply to you:

1 I smoke because I enjoy smoking. ☐

2 I smoke because I have always smoked. ☐

3 I smoke because it helps me to relax. ☐

4 I smoke because it helps me to concentrate. ☐

5 I smoke because it helps me to fit in. ☐

How cigarettes control you

Addiction is clever – it makes you think that you like being under its thumb. But take a good long look at yourself in the mirror. Do you like being controlled in this way?

Most smokers admit to feeling powerless under the spell of nicotine. This is no way to enjoy life. You may say simply that you enjoy smoking – but what do the people close to you think? Your partner may not like it, and children hate being in a smoky atmosphere.

Think about how people close to you feel.

Activity
Why do you smoke?

- In your notebook, write down any other reasons for smoking that you can think of. The purpose of this is to get you thinking about your personal reasons. Scribble down anything that comes into your head. It doesn't matter how far-fetched, silly or irrelevant it may seem. If it springs to mind while you're thinking about smoking, write it down.

- Carry the list around in your pocket and add any extra reasons you think of. Having an understanding of why you smoke will help you to see that there are other ways of fulfilling what smoking provides.

- Throughout the 100-day programme we'll learn how the reasons you think you smoke can be easily discredited.

TOP TIP

Aromatherapy
- Aromatherapists don't claim that they can wean you off cigarettes, but a massage with natural oils can be useful when you give up. The oils smell beautiful and, as you relax, you can breathe in the scents and compare them to a smoky ashtray. There's no question which you'll prefer!

GETTING READY

If you've tried to give up smoking before and found the cravings impossible to survive, it's natural you'll be concerned about this happening again. Every person is different, so it makes sense that different things will work for different people. Some lucky people even give up without experiencing any withdrawal symptoms at all. If you prove to be one of these – make sure that you stop and stay stopped. You never know if you'd feel the same another time.

Willpower

We all know what it feels like to battle against doing something we have an urge to do. We've already seen that the numbers of people who manage to give up smoking on willpower alone are relatively small. Sometimes, it's so hard that it's best not to battle at all. This doesn't mean giving in to temptation, however. It simply means changing the circumstances that are causing the craving. If you're in the pub with friends, for example, rather than using willpower not to smoke, simply leave early, or explain the situation and go for a walk around the block. Remind yourself that it won't always be like this. The need to use these sorts of tactics should only last a few weeks. Before long your willpower *will* be able to cope in challenging situations (as the physical addiction lessens) – and as time goes on, you won't even think about needing willpower.

No more excuses!

Throughout this programme, *No more excuses!* reveals the myths behind some of the common reasons smokers give for continuing their bad habit.

(1) I smoke because I like the taste.

Take a few moments to think back to the first cigarette you smoked. You may associate that time with being young or with a particular group of friends that you remember fondly. But nobody likes the taste of their first cigarette. It's not surprising, now we've seen what's in them. In addition to the poisons, manufacturers often add ingredients like vanilla, honey and chocolate into cigarette paper to sweeten what is really a bitter, caustic taste.

Activity

Danger zones

Make a list of what you think will be your danger zones or weak points. Maybe you always go out after work on a Friday night and have a few drinks and cigarettes, or perhaps you routinely sit with a coffee and a fag once you've dropped the kids at school. Plan how you will avoid these situations and write your plans alongside your danger zones, like this.

Danger zone	Plan
Cig at bus stop on way to work	Will walk to next bus stop
Cig last thing at night	Will go outside for breath of fresh air

TOP TIP

- Treat your taste buds! Once you've given up, why not take a wine-tasting course, learn to cook or spend the money you save on trying a different restaurant every week? Non-smokers have far more sophisticated palates than smokers and can appreciate more subtle flavours.

'All personal achievement starts in the mind of the individual. Your personal achievement starts in your mind. The first step is to know exactly what your problem, goal or desire is.' W. Clement Stone, motivational speaker

GETTING READY

Now that you've decided on your Quit Day, there are some preparations you can make at home in the days before you stop.

1 Don't empty your ashtrays for 24 hours before your Quit Day. Even if the ash spills onto the table or onto the carpet, leave them overflowing to remind yourself just how many you get through in a day.
2 Put a few spare butts in a jam jar half full of water and screw the lid on tight. Put the jar at the back of a kitchen cupboard. If you struggle in the first few days or weeks that you've stopped, take out the jar and put your nose in it – it should put you off!
3 This week, don't put all your clothes straight into the wash. Put a shirt or blouse that you can manage without in a plastic bag at the back of your wardrobe. Open it up a few days after your Quit Day – you'll be amazed how strong the stale smoke smells.

Did you know?

The hit provided when nicotine enters your body is so fast and so concentrated that it creates a higher dependency than heroin. To satisfy the body's need for this level of nicotine concentration, the addicted smoker needs to top up within two hours. But overnight, levels drop to almost that of a non-smoker, which proves that although nicotine is powerful, your body can manage without it.

Ring the changes

You may not even realise it, but your subconscious mind associates smoking with fixed points in your daily routine. Over the next few weeks you'll work towards building a new routine that will become as familiar in the long term as your smoking routine is now. Even making small adjustments can help break patterns that have been fixed for years.

For example, if you always sit at the kitchen table watching breakfast TV with a fag and your first cup of coffee, think about taking your coffee back to bed. Draw open the curtains, prop yourself on your pillows and listen to the radio instead.

Activity

Smoking at home

Think about where you smoke in the home.

Can you list three other changes you can make?

1 ....
....
....

2 ....
....
....

3 ....
....
....

By now, you should be feeling used to the idea that you won't be smoking a cigarette tomorrow. Different people will feel different at this stage – but there are some practical tips that everyone can draw on.

DO

◆ Keep a positive message in your head. You are taking steps towards a new, better life.

◆ Write a few words in your notebook to look at throughout the day tomorrow.

◆ These should remind you *why* you have stopped smoking.

◆ Remember that, even if withdrawal symptoms are tough, they don't last forever.

DON'T

◆ Make a big deal of your last cigarette. Setting a midnight deadline, for example, will only increase pressure on yourself.

◆ Listen to anyone who tries to get you to postpone your Quit Day.

◆ Forget that if you *don't* start tomorrow, you'll only have to do it in the future. You might as well go for it now!

Before you go to bed

◆ Clear out those overflowing ashtrays. Wash them, then throw them away or put them in a bag for the charity shop.

◆ Change your bedding for crisp, clean sheets.

◆ Have a relaxing bath, wash your hair and feel squeaky clean!

◆ Floss your teeth and clean them really well. Gargle with your mouthwash.

◆ Sleep tight!

GETTING READY

Activity

Get rid of the fags!

1 Ensure you have a well-stocked fridge, so you can get up tomorrow and look forward to the breakfast you'll enjoy in place of your normal cigarette. (This doesn't mean pancakes piled high with butter and syrup!)

2 Towards the end of the day, you must dispose of all your leftover cigarettes properly. It's no good putting them in a cupboard or asking your partner or flatmate to hide them. They have to go – FOR GOOD.

   ● Break them in half, near the filter.

   ● Run them under a cold tap until they're soaked through and throw them in the bin.

   ● Keeping a few fags by for 'emergencies' shows you aren't committed.

3 Write a checklist in your notebook. Have you got everything you need for tomorrow, e.g. NRT gum?

'If you can dream it, you can do it.' Walt Disney, film maker

GETTING READY

Your notes

CHAPTER 2

THE FIRST FORTNIGHT

Today is Quit Day. It's important to keep busy and distract yourself from the feeling of wanting a cigarette.

This time tomorrow, you won't have smoked for 24 hours. Can you remember the last time you went without a cigarette for that long? How do you think you'll feel if you manage not to smoke for 24 hours? Write down five *positive* words in your notebook.

Your body is already beginning to respond to you not smoking.

After 8 hours...

◆ Carbon monoxide levels in your bloodstream have already halved.

Try to stick with people who don't smoke today. It's important to distract yourself from your normal smoking routine. It doesn't matter what you do, but plan ahead to give yourself the best chance of tackling cravings.

Activity

Keeping on the straight and narrow

● What are you going to do instead of smoking the first cigarette of the day?

● What are you going to do at lunchtime?

● What things do you have with you to distract you from cravings?

In particular this week you need to plan your evenings. Going to the pub will seriously test your motivation, and if you usually watch television at home you'll be making life hard for yourself too. Get out your smoking notebook and make a list of things to do for every evening for the next week. Try to choose activities where you can't smoke – like going for a swim or to the cinema. Filling your time with practical and enjoyable activities will lead to an all-round confidence boost. You'll feel good that you're shaking up your life and not stuck in the rut of your normal routine. You can get some of those household chores done too.

Divide the page into two columns. Head up the columns:

Need to do	**Want to do**
1 Clean out the car.	Go to a movie.
2	....
3	....
4	....
5	....
6	....
7	....

Be realistic about your tasks. You're more likely to achieve the goal of 'Visit a friend' than you are to go for a six-mile run! Tick the things off the list as you go along.

Keeping a record of your achievements will allow you to look back on your progress and see all the things you have done as a non-smoker.

So you haven't had a cigarette for 24 hours – well done!

'Lead me not into temptation. I can find the way myself.'
Rita Mae Brown, writer

Cravings

Nicotine is a drug. It is one of the most addictive substances known to man, so it's not surprising your body complains when it's deprived of it. This is what happens when you smoke a cigarette:

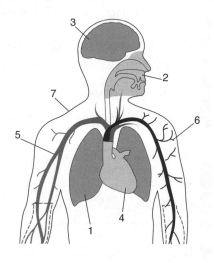

1 **Lungs**. Your lungs need to be clean if they are to function properly. Smoking cigarettes damages the delicate tissue in the lungs. When you smoke, you cough up mucus, which traps bacteria and can lead to you contracting nasty viruses.

2 **Eyes, nose and throat**. An irritating smokers cough is caused by the gases in cigarette smoke. These gases (formaldehyde and ammonia are just two of them), make your eyes, nose and throat sore.

3 **Brain**. Nicotine hits the brain and central nervous system within eight seconds of the first puff. This increases blood pressure, meaning the heart has to work overtime to take in oxygen.

4 **Heart**. Smoke in your lungs forces your heart to work harder. If you smoke for ten minutes, your heart rate could go up as much as 30 per cent. Many smokers suffer from abnormal heartbeats.

5 **Bloodstream**. Carbon monoxide from cigarettes poisons your blood stream. It is the same gas that is found in exhaust fumes and you wouldn't want to inhale those! Carbon monoxide makes it difficult for your red blood cells to carry oxygen. Without oxygen, your body's energy levels are reduced.

6 **Blood vessels**. You're putting stress on your blood vessels, increasing your risk of heart attack as your blood pressure increases.

7 **Skin**. The smoke restricts blood vessels in your skin and dries it out. You're going to get wrinkly.

The impact of nicotine is so fierce, that first-time smokers usually feel sick. But having stopped, your body is continuing to undergo changes.

After 24 hours…

◆ There is *no* carbon monoxide left in your blood.
◆ Your lungs are beginning to clear out mucus and other smoking debris.

TOP TIP

● Although it may be tempting to cut down on cigarettes gradually rather than stopping completely, experts advise against it. If you smoke fewer cigarettes, you're likely to inhale more intensively, which is just as bad for you.

THE FIRST FORTNIGHT

You're doing well. You're slap bang in the middle of the hardest section of this book and you're hanging in there. Today is an important day because …

After 48 hours…

◆ Nicotine is eliminated from the body.

Cravings

Most cravings will come and go over a period of a few days and gradually diminish over a few weeks. Everybody will be affected differently, so don't take too much notice of people who want to tell you 'how it was for them'.

Cravings tend to last between three and five minutes and may be very strong. Have a look at the list below. Which of these suggestions have you already put into practice when you crave a cigarette? Are there any others you could use over the next few days?

◆ Confront cravings head on and prove how determined you are.
◆ Think how much you want to give up. The responsibility is yours and yours alone.
◆ Distract yourself – in any way you know how.
◆ Take three or four deep breaths. Breathe in slowly through the nose and fill your lungs, then breathe out again slowly through the mouth.

THE FIRST FORTNIGHT

◆ Go for a short walk – even if it is just around your workplace.

◆ Read your no-smoking notebook. It will remind you why you are giving up.

◆ Remember – the craving might be strong, but it won't last for long. Think how bad you'll feel if you have a fag, when if you'd just held out for a few more minutes, the craving would have subsided and your resolve would have strengthened.

Activity
Finding a mantra

Think of a mantra that you can repeat to yourself over and over again when you crave a cigarette. It could be something like:

'The craving will pass, the craving will pass, the craving will pass ...'

or:

'I'll feel so good if don't have one, I'll feel so good if I don't have one, I'll feel so good if I don't have one ...'

Learn your mantra. Stick to it. And call on it constantly throughout the programme.

Having not smoked for a few days now, you should be able to begin to establish a pattern of your most vulnerable moments, when cravings hit you hardest. Perhaps it's waiting at the bus stop, the drive to work or your morning coffee break. Being aware of these times should mean you can catch them out before they catch you out. Remember, it's important to break the habit of smoking in particular places and at particular times. You need to keep thinking of small ways in which you can avoid situations that are likely to trigger cravings.

Why not take a different route to work, try tea or hot chocolate in the morning or change the radio programme you listen to in the car? Even small alterations will help with the process of disassociation.

Keep reminding yourself that what you're doing is tough – you've done fantastically well so far.

After 72 hours...

♦ Your bronchial tubes begin to relax, making breathing easier.

Side-effects

The first days are often the hardest, but things typically start to get better after four or five days – and you've already done three! Nicotine withdrawal may make you:

♦ restless
♦ irritable
♦ frustrated
♦ anxious
♦ sleepless.

But remember – all these symptoms will pass. Some people report other side-effects, but don't be alarmed by them – your body is undergoing a physical change and will adjust. These may include:

- clumsiness
- being accident prone
- increased hunger or thirst levels
- indigestion
- nausea
- diarrhoea
- constipation
- headaches.

You may even develop a cough, which will seem odd if you didn't have one while you were smoking. This is caused by the regrowth of cilia (tiny hairs) that line your lungs, clearing out tar and mucus.

Activity

A relaxation technique

This is a simple relaxation technique that you can call on anytime – at home in a quiet room with the lights turned down, or in a crowd if you need to calm yourself or when you are irritable. Use it whenever you feel tense.

Relax:

- Take a good deep breath. Breathe slowly and deeply.

- Let your shoulders droop and sag.

- Unclench your teeth by opening your mouth. Smile if you can or yawn – both release tension.

- Allow the wrinkles in your forehead to unwrinkle.

- Repeat at least three times.

THE FIRST FORTNIGHT

Don't forget to breathe!

This is a great breathing exercise to do first thing in the morning when you wake up. Spend five minutes on it each morning.

1 Lie on your back in bed but don't close your eyes or you might fall back to sleep.
2 Place one hand on your chest and one on your stomach.
3 Breathe in through your nose and allow your stomach to push upwards and outwards. By doing this, you're allowing your diaphragm to expand and air will be pulled deep into your lungs. The upper part of your chest should hardly move.
4 Slowly and evenly breathe out through your nose. Repeat and get a rhythm going. You are aiming to take 8–12 breaths a minute: breathing in and breathing out again counts as one breath.
5 Try to imagine your lungs feeling clean and enjoy the sensation of filling them up with clean, smokeless air.
6 Like yesterday's relaxation exercise, this one can also be used in any situation, and is especially good if you're feeling anxious.

'Breathe. Let go. And remind yourself that this very moment is the only one you know you have for sure.' Oprah Winfrey, TV presenter

Keep reminding yourself why you're giving up

Stopping smoking can make you feel miserable in the short term. If you don't feel strongly motivated, you'll probably have a hard time resisting those cravings. Smokers need to be very clear about their reasons for giving up – motivation should be clear and personal. In other words, we need to know why we're putting ourselves through something very difficult.

You're spending a lot of time this week coping with physical cravings. But giving up smoking has as much to do with the mind as the body, so keep reminding yourself why you've stopped.

Activity

Now versus then

For today's task, draw a comparison with the person you were when you *first started* smoking and the person you are today. Write up your thoughts in your notebook. You may find that the reasons you started are irrelevant to your life now.

Answer these questions to get started.

- How old were you when you began smoking, and how old are you now?
- Why did you begin smoking?
- Do those reasons still apply?
- How have you changed as a person since you began smoking?

Did you know?

- 70 per cent of smokers in the UK would like to stop smoking.
- Most take an average of six times to quit for good.
- But the good news is – however addicted you think you are – it can be done.
- And you're well on your way!

Struggling to give up

Many smokers undergo painful and intrusive operations after developing cancer as a result of smoking. What's shocking is that according to research, 40 per cent of patients who have their larynx removed try smoking again within weeks of the surgery. 50 per cent of lung cancer patients who've had surgery also begin again.

Do you really want to be like that?

THE FIRST FORTNIGHT

Support from family and friends

How do you feel you're doing for support from people around you? When you embark on a stop smoking plan, it's best to ensure you only enlist the help of people you know have your best interests at heart. Friends who are smokers may not be your most enthusiastic supporters. As more and more people give up, smokers feel the uncomfortable consequences of being in a minority. They may even tell you not to bother, or appeal to the side of you that craves a cigarette by telling you that 'one won't hurt'. Don't listen to them! YOU made the decision to stop, even if you have moments of wondering why!

Singles

If you can find someone to quit with, great. You'll be able to encourage each other, knowing that you are sharing many of the same experiences. Otherwise, choose one non-smoking friend or relative who won't mind you calling them to let off steam when the going gets tough. There are plenty of online websites where you can share your progress in a daily blog. Just type 'giving up smoking' into a search engine and browse until you find a site you like the look of.

Partners

If you have a partner, explain that you're serious about giving up and ask him or her to be understanding if withdrawal makes you cranky or miserable for a while. It might help to set aside five minutes a day when you can discuss how you're feeling, but try to limit the amount of time you spend talking about how hard it is. Not only will it try the patience of your partner, but the more you talk about smoking, the less chance your mind has of being distracted onto other topics.

Children

Children are taught about the bad effects of smoking in school and are usually enthusiastic about their parents stopping. Showing them some of the exercises you're doing and reading your no-smoking notebook together will make your efforts a shared experience. Children can be a great help during the 100-day programme. They tend to enjoy the responsibility of being included in an adult project, and if they're helping you, abandoning your plans will be harder.

⊚⚞ TOP TIP

- Ask your children, grandchildren or friends' children to encourage you by drawing a picture that will help you through the programme. Pin it somewhere where you'll see it every day, to remind you that what you're doing is a good example to the next generation.

Activity Support buddies

Decide who your confidantes will be during the 100-day programme. Call them and ask if they are happy to help you. You don't need to talk about giving up smoking incessantly. Two or three friends or colleagues to share your feelings with will be plenty.

'When the going gets tough, the tough get going.'
Joseph P. Kennedy, US Navy pilot

Did you know?

If you manage to stop smoking before middle age, you can avoid 90 per cent of the cancer risks associated with cigarettes.

THE FIRST FORTNIGHT

You're approaching a goal. You are just a day away from having completed a whole week without smoking! Ultimately, QD +88 is your target – but that will seem a very long way off. There's no harm in imagining how great it will feel to get there. In fact, take a few minutes now to think …

1 What a relief it will be to not obsess about cigarettes every minute of the day.
2 How you'll be able to enjoy a drink without worrying if you'll be tempted to smoke.
3 How nobody will be able to give you dirty looks because you're smoking near them.

Activity

Feelings of relief

What will be your biggest feeling of relief when you get to NS+88?

Write down as many feelings as you can here, or in your notebook.

....

....

....

One day at a time

However, it's best not to look too far into the future when trying to give up smoking. The thought of never smoking again can seem very daunting. Instead, all you have to focus on is getting through one day at a time. And you're already proving you can do that. Lots of ex-smokers adopt this approach. They say, 'I won't have a cigarette, just for today,' which seems an achievable, challenge. By the time they wake up the next morning, the start of a new day gives them the impetus to carry it through one more time. As you clock up your NS days, you're putting more and more distance between yourself now and when you were a smoker. Remember – it will get easier!

TOP TIP

- It doesn't matter if you go to bed at 8 o'clock in the evening just to avoid having a smoke. It might seem strange behaviour if you usually don't hit the sack until midnight, but in the morning, you'll have got through another day. Enjoy it!

'I have a new philosophy. I'm only going to dread one day at a time.' Charles M. Schulz, writer (Peanuts, Charlie Brown)

DO

- ◆ Tell yourself you are just going without for today.
- ◆ Tell yourself that you only have to get to bedtime without a cigarette.
- ◆ Think about the things you will enjoy more, once you've given up.

DON'T

- ◆ Think that you have stopped smoking forever.
- ◆ Tell yourself you will never smoke again.
- ◆ Think about social situations like Christmas and parties where you like to smoke.

No more excuses!

(2) I smoke because it helps with pain.

Sad news or physical pain will have most smokers reaching for the fags, but they won't help. If you're wanting to give up, you'll only feel worse because you smoked when you'd rather not have done. Cigarettes do not heal pain – at best they only mask it for a very short period of time.

THE FIRST FORTNIGHT

You've been a non-smoker for a week! That's an amazing achievement. Keep congratulating yourself. Not only is your body free of nicotine and getting back to being healthy, but you've made a positive mental decision to take control of your life. That takes a lot of guts. Well done.

Whatever you do, don't think it's OK to have 'just one' or sneak a drag on someone else's cigarette to celebrate your successful week. It will make you feel horrible both physically and emotionally, and undo all the effort you've put in.

Eleven million people in the UK have given up smoking and you're on your way to joining them. Be confident you can do it. You're putting a lot of time and energy into making this programme work for you and should be feeling proud of yourself.

TOP TIP

- Look to the future and think of something special you'd like to do once you've given up for good. Having a holiday brochure handy to look at pictures of places you'd like to visit will not only give you something to look forward to, but distract you from cravings as well.

Don't expect the cravings to have gone. Certain triggers will still have you yearning for a fag, but now that you've got this far it would be stupid not to press on. You'll want to begin getting your social life back to normal by now, so watch out for these triggers:

- alcohol
- being around friends who smoke
- situations where you might want a cigarette to feel accepted in a new group.

Did you know?

A house that smells of stale smoke is the second most likely cause of a drop in property price, after structural problems. It could knock as much as £16,000 off the sale price of your home!

Make a list of any more triggers that are personal to you – especially if you know you might be faced with them in the coming week.

1 ....

2 ....

3 ....

Activity

A no-smoking home

Now that your body is clear of all the poisons contained in a cigarette, it's time to remove the effects of smoking from your home. Chuck out the bottle of butts and wash the smoky clothing you left in the laundry basket. Spend five minutes in each room of your house, having a good look at the walls, curtains and furniture.

● Fabric absorbs smoke and smells very stale after a while.

● Nicotine discolours paint and wallpaper and can take the shine off fittings like cushions or lampshades.

In your notebook, make a list of tasks that will improve your environment and set aside time over the next few weeks to do some DIY.

● Curtains and cushion covers can be taken to the dry cleaners.

● Carpets will benefit from a shampoo.

Think about re-decorating. Removing pictures from the wall will show you just how dirty exposed areas have become.

THE FIRST FORTNIGHT

So now you're into the second week of being a non-smoker. You're doing fantastically well. For a lot of people, the worst will be over, but unfortunately, with giving up, there's no means of telling at what point different individuals will begin to find things easier. If you are still struggling, don't give up. It will get easier for you too – you just have to be that bit more determined.

Activity
Saying thank you!

Today's task is to make a point of saying thank you to the people who've been supporting you. Tell them how much they've helped you and ask them to keep it up!

Loss or gain?

People who have never smoked often can't understand the scale of loss smokers feel when they give up their cigarettes. Some ex-smokers have even compared the process of giving up as similar to a bereavement. Cigarettes have probably been a part of your life for a long time (though not for ever, as we'll see in a moment!)

It's true that in the long term you will definitely be gaining all round from stopping, but you're unlikely to feel that for a while yet. When you're feeling down, it's very important to be clear about why you have stopped and what the benefits will be. Try to look forward to the sense of elation ex-smokers feel further down the line. It will happen for you and it will be worth it.

No more excuses!

(3) I smoke because I've always smoked.

No you haven't. How old were you when you began smoking? When you were a child, before you'd had your first cigarette, did you yearn for one? No. You've already spent many years of your life as a non-smoker.

Remember, it's not surprising if you are missing your cigarettes. Read through your notebook whenever you experience that sense of loss. You'll see that you made the decision to give up for good reasons.

Most people start smoking in their teens for social reasons but, as you know, smoking quickly becomes connected with specific feelings and situations. You've made the break, but you need to keep working on getting rid of this emotional attachment, which can take time.

Some things you might be missing

Smoking can be:

♦ a particular part of your daily life
♦ your way of dealing with stress and difficult situations
♦ something you think of as an aid to concentration
♦ a reward
♦ a way to pass the time
♦ a means of introduction and meeting new friends
♦ a way to feel part of a group
♦ a 'do not disturb sign'
♦ a habit
♦ an enjoyable ritual
♦ a part of your identity.

Activity

Your relationship with smoking

Study the list and think about your own relationship with smoking. Tick the things on the list that you are missing most or that have the most relevance to how you are feeling. It's important that you keep reminding yourself of the psychological ties you have with cigarettes. If you work out what smoking means to you and are aware of your triggers, it will make the next few days and weeks easier.

TOP TIP

- Remember, any symptoms you may be experiencing are not a result of giving up. They are the symptoms caused by smoking.

Causes of death annually in the UK

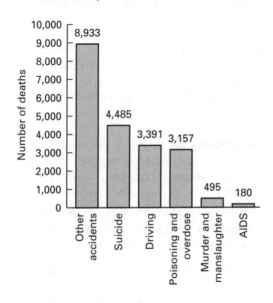

Smoking kills around 120,000 people each year. The figure is so much higher than any of the other causes of death that it can't be fitted on the graph.

'Frustration, although quite painful at times, is a very positive and essential part of success.' Bo Bennett, writer

Yesterday, you thought about some of the things you've been missing since you gave up smoking. Today, you have to show yourself that you have the brainpower to overcome that sense of loss. See if you can come up with practical solutions for them all. You may already have begun to think of ways to cope.

Activity

Solve your problems

This is a problem-solving activity. Following the example below, work through the list until you have solutions to each of the problems you may be facing. Once you've written them down, they will be always be there for you to refer back to when the going gets tough.

Example: Smoking as a part of daily life
Smokers often use cigarettes to punctuate their day. A cigarette between tasks marks the point at which you finish one thing and move on to another.

'To overcome this I have found a new way of marking changes. I make a cup of herbal tea instead of having a coffee and a fag.'

1 Smoking as a way to cope with difficult situations
Smoking can be a way to moderate negative feelings such as stress, nervousness and anxiety.

'To overcome this I will ...'

2 Smoking when I need to concentrate
Lapses in concentration affect around 60 per cent of smokers and usually lasts for less than two weeks, according to ASH.

'To overcome this I will ...'

3 Smoking is my reward
Smokers often use tobacco as both reward and motivator – for example, before a boring task or at the end of a hard day.

'To overcome this I will ...'

4 Smoking passes the time
In many situations, smoking fills in breaks and passes the time, especially 'dull' time such as sitting in a traffic jam.

'To overcome this I will ...'

5 Company and communication
Tobacco can be a good way of meeting new people. Asking for a light or sharing matches can provide an easy opportunity to talk to strangers.

'To overcome this I will ...'

6 Smoking and friendship
Smoking can make you feel part of a group, especially at work.

'To overcome this I will ...'

7 Smoking is an effective 'do not disturb' sign
Few people will interrupt someone who's smoking, or ask them to put down their cigarette in a hurry. You will need to find other ways of signalling to colleagues and family that you don't want to be disturbed.

'To overcome this I will ...'

8 Breaking the habit of smoking
It's such a habit, I get a sudden impulse for a cigarette when the phone rings or I check my emails.

'To overcome this I will ...'

9 Breaking rituals
Over time you've built up small rituals, for example, the way you open a packet, hold a cigarette or exhale smoke. If you've given up pipe smoking or used to smoke roll-ups, this is what you might miss most.

'To overcome this I will ...'

10 Smoking and identity
The label 'smoker' can be an integral part of your image. When you quit you have to let go of these perceptions – especially if you started smoking at an early age.

'To overcome this I will ...'

Remember – time spent working on activities and tasks in this book is time spent not smoking!

THE FIRST FORTNIGHT

Did you know?

British smokers claim to smoke 14 fags a day on average. (Most admit the count goes up the more alcohol they drink.) 15 per cent have their first fag of the day within five minutes of waking up. 46 per cent wait until they've been awake for half an hour.

How desperate is that?!

Try not to dwell on the negative aspects of how you're feeling. It's fine to acknoweldge them as part of the process of letting go, but make sure you think about the good things too. Try to follow up every negative thought with a positive thought and it will become a habit. Without realising it, your outlook will become more positive as a result of thinking good thoughts. This will make the difficult moments easier to tackle.

For example, each time you think, 'I'm desperate for a fag', force yourself to follow up that thought with, 'But when the craving wears off, I'm going to feel great that I didn't have one.'

'A strong positive mental attitude will create more miracles than any wonder-drug.' Patricia Neal, actress

No more excuses!

④ **I smoke because I'm afraid I won't cope with the withdrawal symptoms of giving up.**

Fear of the hardship of giving up puts a lot of people off taking the first steps, especially if you've tried before. But remember – plenty of people have a few goes at stopping before they crack it for good. It's always better to keep trying than not to try at all. You're already at NS+11, so you've proved you can go without a fag on a daily basis, which is all you have to manage.

Some people following the programme might even be pleasantly surprised. If you've thought long and hard about stopping, the reality can actually be easier than the build up.

Activity The benefits of not smoking

Stopping smoking will enable you to have more:

Key:

Fun

Money

Confidence

Energy

Pride

Enthusiasm

A	F	J	U	T	H	S	W	E	T	O
E	R	H	A	W	Y	D	U	I	R	P
H	N	R	T	E	S	E	W	A	V	N
P	B	T	O	Y	I	C	N	C	Q	U
A	D	U	H	W	O	N	P	O	C	M
O	I	R	D	U	B	E	Y	F	M	R
F	Y	E	S	C	S	D	N	B	E	P
F	U	N	I	E	D	I	R	P	A	C
A	D	E	R	U	G	F	A	A	S	J
D	A	R	C	B	T	N	W	S	E	O
V	D	G	E	F	S	O	K	H	M	C
J	I	Y	E	W	A	C	V	I	A	F

See how long it takes you to spot these five benefits in the word puzzle.

Words can be run backwards, forwards, up and down or diagaonally.

According to ASH, smokers who smoke between 1 and 14 cigarettes a day are eight times more likely to die from lung cancer than non-smokers.

It would be great if there was a quick fix to giving up smoking – if you could throw away your fags one day and never feel like having one again. But, like most rewarding things in life, the transition takes time, effort and determination. You may be finding that the cravings you experience are a little less intense than in the first few days, but it's also possible that – now you've got this far – the novelty of managing to stop is wearing off.

It's especially important from now on to be extra vigilant about resisting cigarettes.

You are still vulnerable. The good news is that you've stopped smoking for long enough to be able to appreciate some of the practical advantages of your achievements so far. You need incentives to keep you going at this time – and a good incentive to start with is how much money you're saving.

Counting the cost

When you were smoking, you probably tried not to think too hard about what it was costing you on a daily basis – but it will have been a lot! If you smoked 20 a day for a lifetime, the total would be almost £100,000!

Activity

Saving money

If someone gave you that amount of money right now what would you spend it on?

....

Of course, giving up the fags won't result in a lump sum. So, for today's task ...

- Find a jar that will become your no-smoking piggy bank. A transparent container will work best because it will enable you to see how much you've saved.

- Work out how much you were spending on cigarettes each day or each week.

- Put the money you're saving in the container instead.

- Continue to do this throughout the 100-day programme.

TOP TIP

- Don't slip into a habit of using your cash jar as a handy cash point machine – and ask your family to appreciate its symbolic significance too. Dipping into the jar will undermine its purpose. The point is to watch your savings grow – all the time making a visual connection with the contents of the jar, and the fact you're not smoking.

The chart below should help you count the cost of smoking, based upon an average price of £4.82 per pack of 20 cigarettes (2005 prices).

The cost of smoking					
Cigarettes per day	1 year	5 years	10 years	20 years	Lifetime (est. 56 years of smoking)
10	£880	£4,401	£8,803	£17,605	£49,294
20	£1,761	£8,803	£17,605	£35,210	£98,588
30	£2,641	£13,204	£26,408	£52,815	£147,882
40	£3,521	£17,605	£35,210	£70,420	£197,177
60	£5,282	£26,408	£52,815	£105,630	£295,765

THE FIRST FORTNIGHT

The incentive of being able to treat yourself and your family to something special as a result of giving up smoking should grow stronger as you see your piggy bank filling up. But you can also feel good for lots of other financial reasons.

Tax

Taxes on cigarettes are high and will continue to get higher every time a new governmental budget is announced.

◆ In Canada, cigarette smoking fell by between 50 per cent and 60 per cent when prices were significantly increased in the late 1980s and early 1990s.
◆ In the UK, a packet of 20 cigarettes cost £1.85 in 1971 and the average smoker got through 15,000 fags that year.
◆ By 1995, the price was around £2.65 a pack, and the average smoker's annual consumption had dropped to 10,000.
◆ If you smoke 20 a day, you'll be getting through 7,200 fags a year.

Quantities of cigarettes imported and exported, UK (2002–2003)

54,737 million cigarettes released
for consumption in the UK

10.4 billion imported into the UK

72.3 billion cigarettes released for consumption in the UK

Source: ASH

'There is absolutely clear evidence that higher prices reduce consumption, especially among young people. It's the one tax that can help you avoid death'. World Health Organization.

Today is another significant landmark. At Day 25 you are a quarter of the way through the 100-day programme.

Activity
Enjoy a walk

Go for a walk today. If you live in a city choose your favourite park. If you live in the countryside find a path that takes you through pretty scenery.

● Walk briskly for at least half an hour.

● Swing your arms.

● Breathe deeply and think how your lungs are enjoying the fresh air.

● Take in the sky and the trees.

● Enjoy looking at the world in a new way.

Did you know?

Cigarettes act as a form of self-medication. They can blunt how you really feel. So it's normal to feel moods and emotions more deeply when you give up smoking. Ask people to be patient with you if you find you're getting upset or angry more than usual.

THE FIRST FORTNIGHT

All the tasks and activities you've completed so far in the 100-day programme have been geared toward distracting you from smoking. You've learned to think about why you smoke and what your weak points are. You've devised ways to divert your attention when you crave a cigarette. You've picked up tips to reinforce your motivation when you're flagging and think ahead to the happy non-smoker you'll be in the future.

In an ideal world, you'll never smoke a cigarette again. But let's be realistic. It's well known that plenty of people make more than one attempt to quit, before they succeed for good.

For the new non-smoker, relapses are often a part of life, so it makes sense to have a coping strategy to refer to if and when it happens.

 TOP TIP

- The most important thing if you do have a cigarette after your Quit Day is not to panic. It's not the end of the world!

It's important that you follow these points.

DO

- ◆ Throw away any evidence of your relapse, i.e. leftover cigarettes and butts.
- ◆ Have a shower, clean your teeth and wash the clothes you were wearing.
- ◆ Drink a glass of fresh juice and eat healthy, fresh food all day.
- ◆ Exercise today. Go to the gym or a long walk.
- ◆ Think about the circumstances that caused the relapse and how you can avoid falling into the same trap again.
- ◆ Read through your no-smoking notebook. Think of it as extra homework that you're doing, because you didn't get the grade you deserved first time around.
- ◆ Put it behind you – pick yourself up and carry on.

DON'T

◆ Think, 'I've blown it, so I might as well carry on smoking.'
◆ Let one slip-up undo all your hard work.
◆ Beat yourself up about having relapsed.

These rules apply whether you had one crafty fag in a stressful moment, or went on a complete bender and smoked a whole pack. Remember – never give up giving up!

'I've failed over and over and over again in my life and that is why I succeed.' Michael Jordan, basketball star

Activity

Get angry!

Get angry! – but don't get angry with yourself. You can direct your anger elsewhere!

1 Get angry at the government for making billions of pounds from tobacco taxes and not spending the income as you'd like it spent.

2 Get angry at tobacco companies who spend billions on marketing campaigns to try to keep you smoking and target vulnerable people in poor countries.

3 Get angry with the people who believe smokers should go to the back of the queue for hospital treatment, when the tax you pay for cigarettes part-funds the NHS.

4 Get angry at insurance companies who hike their premiums for smokers. Somebody who smokes one a month is treated the same as somebody on 40 a day!

Now, take a few deep breaths. You've stopped smoking. You don't need to get angry any more. These things no longer concern you. You can get on with thinking about your positive and healthy future.

THE FIRST FORTNIGHT

Your notes

CHAPTER 3

STAYING STOPPED

Hopefully, you enjoyed a good walk earlier in the week. If it put you in the mood for more exercise, that's great. Now that your body is clear of nicotine and your lungs and heart are beginning to recover, it's time to think about boosting your overall health.

An American study has found that smokers who exercise while trying to kick the habit are more than twice as likely to succeed. Giving up cigarettes may give you the boost you need to join a gym or go jogging. But if you're not the sporty type, don't worry. There are plenty of ways that exercise can be incorporated into your daily life.

Activity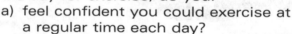

Are you a hare or a tortoise?

This quiz will help you to decide the type of exercise programme that will suit you:

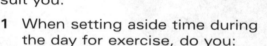

1 When setting aside time during the day for exercise, do you:
   a) feel confident you could exercise at a regular time each day?
   b) feel worried there's not enough time in your schedule?

2 When you decide to try out a new activity do you:
   a) throw yourself into it full on, as soon as you can?
   b) research, plan and buy any necessary equipment before beginning?

3 Are you the kind of person who:
   a) measures progress in gradual achievements?
   b) likes instant results?

4 In general, how successful are you at changing your habits and routines?
   a) I am successful.
   b) I struggle to change.

5 Which reason for exercise appeals to you most?
   a) It will improve my looks.
   b) It will improve my health.

6 In what kind of situation do you perform best?
   a) Projects that require taking one step at a time.
   b) Projects that require bursts of activity.

7 Which statement best sums up your exercise goals?
   a) Work hard and get fit quick.
   b) Slow and steady improvements towards sustainable health.

8 When you have to wait for something to happen do you:
   a) bide your time patiently?
   b) feel stressed and impatient?

9 Who has most inspired you to begin exercising?
   a) Yourself.
   b) Family, friends or doctor.

Your score:

If you scored mostly Bs – you're more of a hare than a tortoise.

If you scored mostly As – you're more of a tortoise than a hare.

It doesn't matter which category you fall into. There are all sorts of exercises to suit all sorts of people. The important thing is to find something you'll enjoy – and be able to stick with.

CHECK ✔

This week I have:

◆ done a breathing exercise every day to overcome cravings.

(Day 16 will show you how!)

STAYING STOPPED

Exercise has the following physical benefits:

◆ It increases levels of HDL or 'good' cholesterol in the body.
◆ It lowers blood pressure.
◆ It burns fat, which can change the shape of your body.
◆ It helps maintain blood sugar levels.
◆ It boosts the immune system.
◆ It promotes strength and bone density.

When you begin an exercise programme as part of giving up smoking, it can have a profound psychological impact:

◆ You'll feel good for taking another positive step toward becoming a healthy non-smoker.
◆ You're less likely to crave a cigarette if you've just spent an hour working out.
◆ You'll have a new purpose in your life and a new routine.
◆ You'll be around people who are interested in good health and less likely to be smokers.
◆ You can develop a new social circle.
◆ The hormones induced through exercise boost your mood and lessen the chances of depression.

Hares

If you're a hare think about joining a local netball, hockey or football team or a running club. Other people will be relying on you if you join a team, so it's a good way to commit to regular exercise. But you could also go to the gym or go cycling.

Tortoises

If you're not used to exercising it can seem daunting, but don't make excuses. Nobody is expecting you to dress in lycra and enter a marathon!

Make a commitment to introduce walking into your daily routine. Half an hour, at a brisk pace, swinging your arms, will do you a world of good if you haven't done it before on a regular basis. If you usually catch the bus to work, get off two stops early and walk the rest of the way.

- Walk up escalators and take the stairs instead of the lift.
- Gardening gives you fresh air as well as exercise.
- You can even speed up doing your housework for an extra activity boost.
- Before you get in the car, think whether your journey could be made on foot.
- Swimming is great exercise and most pools have at least some spa facilities these days. Treat yourself to a sauna or a massage after you've done your lengths. (Yes, you can afford it – with the money you've saved from cigarettes!)

Activity

Set an exercise goal

Set yourself an exercise goal for this week. Be clear about what you want to achieve and write it in your notebook to tick off when you've completed it.

Three good examples

- After work three evenings this week, I will set aside an hour to go for a walk. I will ask (name a friend or relative) to come with me, so we can chat and catch up on our news at the same time as exercising.

- On Saturday, I will do an hour's gardening/wash the car/spring clean the kitchen.

- I will get up half an hour early on Sunday morning and walk to buy a newspaper from a shop that is further away than my usual newsagent.

STAYING STOPPED

Throughout the 100-day programme, you're building a new lifestyle.

Sticking to an exercise programme requires motivation in the same way that giving up smoking does. Try to think of the two as ongoing processes that compliment each other. You are learning new skills that should last you a lifetime. With exercise, as with not smoking, take one day at a time. Introduce activity gradually and, over time, it will become a natural part of your everyday life. It shouldn't seem like an ordeal.

How much exercise is enough?

Half an hour of moderately intense exercise, most days of the week, is the Department of Health's recommended quota. This is the equivalent of a brisk walk for 30 minutes. If you don't have any long-term health problems and are steady on your feet, you should be able to manage it.

- Motivation

- Patience

- Pacing

- Commitment

These are the four major aspects of every exercise programme.

No more excuses!

⑤ **I smoke because it controls my weight.**

Some people do feel less hungry after a cigarette. But remember, plenty of non-smokers are happy with their weight and plenty of smokers are overweight. It's not impossible to be a non-smoker and stay trim. Research has shown that smokers' metabolisms are artificially speeded up, which means their bodies don't absorb nutrients properly.

STAYING STOPPED

Weight gain

Fear of gaining weight is one of the main reasons that women, in particular, give for not stopping smoking. Combining healthy eating with regular exercise is by far the best way to stay trim.

Activity

See how far you've come

Don't forget to take time to reflect on how far you've come. Sit quietly for ten minutes and recap on your lifestyle changes so far. Do you feel you're coping well with the programme, or could you do with some extra help?

Answer the following questions by writing your feelings in your notebook, or discussing them with a friend:

1   Are you still making small changes to routine habits, as you learned in Chapter 1?

2   Is it easier to cope with your weak spots, for example making a phone call without a cigarette, or not having a fag in your lunch break?

3   Are you feeling pleased with your progress or depressed that you're not smoking?

Remember – you're in control. If you feel you can't cope, go back to your GP, find out about joining a smoking clinic, or research other options like hypnotherapy or acupuncture.

STAYING STOPPED

Every day that's passed since you last smoked has been of benefit to your health.

Between 2 and 21 weeks...

◆ Your circulation begins to improve. Poor circulation causes problems, ranging from persistently cold hands and feet, to slow skin healing, Raynauds disease (restriction of blood vessels in the hands, feet, ears and lips) and peripheral vascular disease (restriction of vessels around the heart and brain).

It's time to check up on how you're coping with withdrawal. Hopefully, the intense side effects you felt in the first few days without nicotine have subsided. The following table shows common longer-term symptoms reported by recent non-smokers.

Column 1 describes the symptom. Column 2 shows how long the symptom lasted on average in the sample group of people used to calculate the findings. (The arrows indicate how long the symptom might last. A left-pointing arrow means 'less than'; a right-pointing arrow means 'more than'.) Column 3 shows how many people in the sample group suffered that particular symptom, for the average duration.

Treat the table as a guide – everybody reacts differently to stopping smoking. But if, for example, you're still sleeping poorly or feeling depressed, it's worth asking your doctor for advice.

Symptom	Duration	Prevalence
Irritability	< 4 weeks	50%
Depression	< 4 weeks	60%
Restlessness	< 4 weeks	60%
Poor concentration	< 2 weeks	60%
Increased appetite	> 10 weeks	70%
Light-headedness	< 48 hours	10%
Insomnia	< 1 week	25%
Urges to smoke	> 2 weeks	70%
Increase in weight	Long term	> 80%

How are you feeling?

When you look at the table, you should be encouraged by the fact that you're not the only one who's had to cope with some difficult withdrawal symptoms. As you can see, a tendency to put on weight comes at the bottom of the list and is experienced by a high number of people for a prolonged period. It's why exercise is such an important part of the 100-day programme.

At QD +18 it's time to get a grip on what you're eating, so that you don't fall into replacing one bad habit (smoking) with another (snacking).

Activity

Check out your food cupboards!

On a kitchen worktop make two piles, one of 'healthy' foods and one 'snack' foods from your cupboards.

Under 'healthy' foods, you can put:
- fruit
- vegetables
- wholemeal breads.

Under 'snack' foods, put:
- biscuits
- sweets and chocolates
- crisps.

Don't worry, there isn't a ban on snack foods. It's just important from now on to monitor how much of them you're eating. If your pile of snack foods is bigger than your pile of healthy foods, you need to redress the balance next time you go to the supermarket.

- Have you noticed that you reach for the biscuit tin instead of having a cigarette?
- Have you been buying sweets in the newsagents instead of cigarettes?

If you answer 'yes' to these questions, break the habit – before it's too late!

STAYING STOPPED

65

The urge to eat more

Everyone feels an increased urge to eat when they first stop smoking. There are two reasons for this.

1 Physical reasons

Nicotine affects the chemistry of your blood in a way that influences appetite:

◆ Inhaling nicotine produces adrenaline, which causes the body to release excess sugar into the bloodstream.
◆ Nicotine inhibits the release of the hormone insulin, which removes excess sugar from the blood.
◆ This means smokers have slightly more sugar in their blood between cigarettes than usual.
◆ Blood sugar acts as an appetite suppressant, meaning smokers don't usually feel hungry as often as non-smokers.

2 Psychological reasons

There are several emotional reasons why recent ex-smokers feel the urge to snack:

Did you know?

The average weight gain among people who give up smoking is 1.8 kg. The health risk of an extra 1.8 kg is much lower than the health risk of smoking. And some people don't put on any weight at all. Don't use weight gain as an excuse for not quitting.

◆ For a long time, you lit a cigarette in reaction to every possible emotion. Good news, bad news, feeling tired or anxious – you reached for a fag every time. It's not surprising you feel lost without them.
◆ Food seems to replace that comforting effect – especially as it tastes much better now it's not covered up with smoke.
◆ Think how many times a day you used to lift your hand to your mouth to inhale a cigarette. The action itself is a habit, which needs to be broken along with all the other habits you're slowly breaking down.

Activity

Keep hunger at bay

Follow these steps today to learn to keep your hunger pangs in check.

1 Pay attention to your body. You'll see that what feels like a hunger pang may be an indicator of something else:
   – anger
   – fatigue
   – boredom.
   ● Don't automatically reach for the biscuits.
   ● Treat the underlying reason.
   ● Use the same skills of distracting yourself that you've learned to avoid having a cigarette.

2 Drink water.
   ● It's a great hunger buster and will flush toxins out of your body.

3 Plan ahead.
   ● Put some healthy snacks together in advance.
   ● If you need something to nibble, having some fruit, nuts or raisins handy will stop you going out to buy chocolate.

4 Avoid worthless calories.
   ● Chips, sweets and ice-cream pile on the pounds but have no nutritional value.
   ● Your body digests them quickly.
   ● Your blood sugar shoots up.
   ● And, just like cigarettes, you'll be craving another hit before you know it because your blood sugar will have plummeted.

Don't give up giving up!

People who give up smoking but then relapse make all sorts of excuses. One is that there was no fun left in life. Not only could they not smoke, but they couldn't eat what they wanted either. Nobody is underestimating how hard it is to stick to the programme. But you can do it.

STAYING STOPPED

It's best to get your eating patterns in check early on in your life as a non-smoker. If you've scoffed a few extra bars of chocolate between QD +1 and today, it won't have done you much harm. But snacking can become a habit just as cigarettes did.

And as we all know now – the best way to give up smoking is ...?

never start!

Get off to a good start!

Smokers often skip meals and – especially at breakfast – just have a coffee and a fag. But this isn't a healthy way to start each day. Why not buy a blender and get into the habit of drinking a fruit smoothie for breakfast? The World Health Organization recommends we eat five portions of fruit and veg a day. A breakfast smoothie will get you halfway there before the day has started – another achievement to make you feel healthy and proud of yourself.

Smoothie recipe

You can use whatever fruit you like in a smoothie – it couldn't be easier! Try:

◆ 1 banana
◆ 1 small handful strawberries/ raspberries/blackberries
◆ 1 sliced peach/pear
◆ 2 spoonfuls yoghurt
◆ 1 cup orange juice

Throw them all in the blender together and switch it on!

- For a change, use milk instead of fruit juice.
- Add nuts, oats or seeds for a bit more bulk.
- A teaspoon of honey will sweeten.
- Keep a few tins of fruit in cupboard to use if you don't have anything fresh.

Activity

Create recipes

- Create your own recipes and have a tasting session.

- Buy some exotic fruits you haven't tasted before.

- Be as imaginative as you like when mixing them together.

- Get your kids, friends or partner involved and have a competition to see who can make the best smoothie!

'Eat breakfast like a king, lunch like a prince and dinner like a pauper.' Adelle Davis, nutritionist

Did you know?

Osteoporosis or 'thinning' of the bones has been found to be associated with smoking. It's a painful, often crippling condition that affects more women than men. Eating a healthy diet – rich in calcium – helps to guard against osteoporosis. Calcium is found in dairy products – even more reason to use that blender!

STAYING STOPPED

If you've got this far into the 100-day programme and not had a cigarette, you're doing brilliantly. It shows you've taken responsibility for your life and are serious about being a non-smoker.

Activity

Start a food diary

Begin a food diary in your notebook. Make a list of everything you eat and drink in a day as you go along. Go through the list in the evening, after your last meal, and see how you could kick your diet into shape. Aim to make one or two changes at a time, until your daily food intake is made up of the following suggestions:

Breakfast	Mid-morning/ Mid-afternoon	Lunch	Dinner
Smoothie	Nuts and raisins	Baked potato	Meat
Cereal	Fruit	Salad	Fish
Toast	Bagel	Veg	Veg
Yogurt	Biscuit	Sandwich	Pudding

You're not on a diet, so nothing is off the menu, but before you tuck into double portions or reach for a bar of chocolate, remember to check what you've already eaten so far that day. Being aware of what you're eating ahead of putting food in your mouth will mean that reaching for unhealthy snacks doesn't become a habit.

There are plenty of ways to enjoy your food without making it a smoking substitute if you follow a few careful rules:

◆ Make sure you're not doubling quantities to stave off cigarette cravings.

◆ Don't go hungry, but fill yourself up with non-fattening foods. Steer clear of saturated fats and processed foods.

◆ Eat as much fruit and veg as you like – they contain important vitamins and minerals.

◆ Boost your calcium intake with low-fat dairy products and fish.

◆ Top up your iron levels with meat, spinach and wholegrains.

◆ Give yourself something to look forward to – a cooked breakfast at the weekend, for example, rather than every day.

◆ Allow yourself one treat a day. Have a biscuit with your morning tea or a bar of chocolate after dinner.

◆ Keep hydrated by sipping water throughout the day. Try to drink eight glasses between getting up in the morning and going to bed at night.

CHECK ✔

This week I have:

◆ reminded myself WHY I gave up smoking by writing down the three main reasons.

1 ....

2 ....

3 ....

In the beginning, you probably found that avoiding social situations and alcohol was a necessary means of not being tempted to smoke. But you want to be able to enjoy seeing friends and having a drink again. This is perfectly possible, as long as you remember that you are still in the danger zone!

Activity

Plan ahead

Check your diary and see what plans you have to meet friends over the next week. The key is to think ahead and prepare yourself mentally for an enjoyable evening that's not going to result in you having a cigarette.

Socialising action plan

An hour before you go out, gather your thoughts. Do a relaxing breathing exercise and tell yourself that, however tempted you are, you are not going to have a cigarette.

If you're going out in a group of non-smokers, tell them that the evening will be hard for you. They will want to encourage and support you if they don't smoke themselves.

Enjoy asking for a non-smoking table – congratulate yourself that you are now able to do this. If you crave a cigarette after dinner, use the skills you have learned to convince yourself that although it's intense, the craving will not last. If other people at the table are smoking, do anything to distract yourself. Go to the bathroom, go outside for a breath of fresh air, or move down the table to talk to someone who's not smoking.

Keep your alcohol intake to a minimum. Enjoy making glass of wine last – and look forward to not waking up with a hangover.

Think ahead to how you will feel when you get home if you have:

a) not smoked (I will feel .... with myself.)

b) smoked (I will feel .... with myself.)

You will feel so proud of yourself if you say goodnight as a non-smoker!

Check your alcohol intake

Maximum three units a day for women.

Maximum four units a day for men – regardless of your size.

| 1/2 pint of ordinary strength beer, larger or cider | 1 small glass of wine | 1 single measure of spirits | 1 small glass of sherry | 1 single measure of apertifs |

No more excuses!

⑥ I smoke because I couldn't imagine drinking alcohol without a cigarette.

Nobody is pretending that breaking this link will be easy, but think about *why* you're more likely to smoke more when you drink.

Alcohol has a numbing effect on the throat, so you're less able to feel the irritant effect when you inhale. But your throat becomes scratched and raw and you've been doing untold damage to its delicate lining.

STAYING STOPPED

We all have an image of how we look – or how we would like to look. If you've been a smoker for a long time, holding a cigarette, asking for a light, leaning back in your chair and inhaling will all be part of your self-image. When you give up, you need to change the way you see yourself.

Activity

Attributes of a smoker

Tick the attributes you think applied to you as a smoker:

- Cool
- Sexy
- Attractive
- Confident
- Relaxed

- Charming
- Rebellious
- Enigmatic
- Outspoken
- Sociable

How many of the ten did you tick? If it was more than one or two, you're seriously misguided.

The wrong image

For years, smoking was associated with all sorts of qualities. You can probably think of popular advertising campaigns featuring rugged cowboys or attractive women. This trend began long before the link between smoking and serious damage to health was established. Once that link was established, tobacco companies designed ever more glamorous campaigns, in order not to lose sales. But if you think for a moment, it's not hard to counter the advertisers' efforts. Smoking makes you look sexy? Ask any non-smoker if they'd rather kiss someone with fresh breath, or someone who smelled and tasted like an ashtray.

Did you know?

In many developing countries:

- There are no health warnings on cigarettes.
- There are no advertising or sponsorship controls.
- Smoking is still portrayed as a sophisticated Western habit, which encourages people to take it up.
- Tobacco companies have been known to give free cigarettes to youngsters, to get them addicted to their brand.
- As people become addicted to tobacco they have less money available for necessities such as food.
- When people get sick, they don't have access to health services as we are used to in wealthy nations.

Think your favourite actor or actress looks good because they smoke?

Remember – they're playing a role. Most celebrities are far too concerned about their looks to smoke in real life.

STAYING STOPPED

In the UK, it's legal to smoke and buy cigarettes from the age of 16. Thousands of people take up smoking in their teens because they don't have the maturity to resist peer pressure.

Teenagers are impressionable – but you're likely to be an adult! You don't need to do what other people want you to do.

Percentage of secondary school children who are regular smokers (at least one cigarette per week on average), England

Age 15	1982	1984	1986	1988	1990	1992	1994	1996	1998	2000	2003
Boys	24	28	18	17	25	21	26	28	19	21	18
Girls	25	28	27	22	25	25	30	33	29	26	26
All	25	28	22	20	25	23	28	30	24	23	22

Source: ASH

Activity
When did you start smoking?

1 Write 200 words (a couple of paragraphs) entitled 'The day I started smoking'. Include the circumstances, who you were with, how you felt and what the cigarette tasted like.

2 Read what you've written out loud – either to yourself or to someone else.

3 Now imagine you're advising a teenager who is about to smoke their first cigarette. What advice will you give them?

4 Listen to your own advice. Use it to make sure you don't give up giving up!

STAYING STOPPED

Set a good example

- Children are three times as likely to smoke if both of their parents smoke.
- Three out of four children are aware of cigarettes by the time they reach the age of five.
- By 11, a third of UK children have tried smoking.
- By 16, two thirds have tried it.
- In the UK, 450 children under the age of 16 begin smoking every day.
- 11 per cent of that age group go on to become regular smokers.

Advice for parents

- Talk to your kids about smoking.
- Share this book with them and explain how you wish you'd never started smoking.
- Remind them how much of their hard-earned money they'll be wasting if they smoke.
- Teenagers often aren't bothered about the dangers to health because they're young and fit. Explain how smoking made you feel and why you're giving up.
- If your kids smoke regularly keep an open discussion going. Encourage them to give up, rather than trying to force the issue.

STAYING STOPPED

Smoking and age

Smoking wipes ten years off a person's life on average, but giving up at any age brings huge benefits.

Age when quit smoking	Years of life gained
60	3
50	6
40	9
30	10

Half of all smokers who don't give up will die as a result of their habit. A quarter of all smokers die in middle-age. You're never too old to give up.

'You often hear people say "I'm 40 now, so it's not worth giving up". But stopping really does work – giving up at 40 means that just one year of life is lost on average, instead of ten.' Professor Richard Peto, University of Oxford

Percentage of smokers (England), per year

	1974	1978	1982	1986	1990	1994	1996	1998	2000	2003
Men	51	45	38	35	31	28	29	28	29	28
Women	41	37	33	31	29	26	28	26	25	24
All	45	40	35	33	30	27	28	27	27	26

Source: ASH

STAYING STOPPED

No more excuses!

(7) My granddad smoked all his life and lived until he was 90.

Of course there are cases like this because every rule has exceptions. But the evidence that smoking kills is overwhelming – and the odds of you living like your granddad are very, very low. It might make you feel better to think you'll be unaffected by smoking – it might make you feel clever to tell your friends it's your reason for not giving up. But it's almost certain that a few years down the line your bravado will be destroyed and you'll develop a chronic illness.

How will you feel then?

Activity

Five-year plan

Remember that question you get asked at job interviews? 'Where would you like to be in five years' time?' Answer it now! You can write down any or all of your ambitions, but you must include 'I want to be a non-smoker'.

....

....

....

....

....

....

STAYING STOPPED

Smoking has a bad effect on every part of the body. It harms you on the inside and the outside. Non-smokers begin to age at around 30 years old. Smokers begin to age the moment they first inhale.

How are you ageing?

Take this quiz to find out:

1 Pinch a fold of skin on the back of your hand. Does it:
   a) spring back into place before you notice?
   b) form a ridge that takes a while to subside?
2 Run a finger nail down the side of your face. What happens?
   a) Flakes of skin come off under your nail.
   b) Your skin feels soft and supple.
3 How often do you use sunscreen when you're not on holiday?
   a) Rarely or never.
   b) If I'm going to be outside in summer, I always slap it on.
4 When you're in a smoky atmosphere do your eyes:
   a) feel irritated and watery?
   b) not notice that the room is full of smoke?
5 How much water do you drink each day?
   a) Five glasses or more.
   b) Fewer than five glasses.
6 If the sun is in your eyes do you:
   a) always have sunglasses handy to put on?
   b) screw up your face and squint to keep the light out?
7 Do you stick to a strict routine of cleansing and moisturising your face morning and evening?
   a) Yes.
   b) No.
8 What essentials would you put in your wash bag if you were going away for a night?
   a) Soap, toothbrush, toothpaste.
   b) Cleanser, moisturiser, toothbrush, toothpaste.

9 Run your fingers through your hair. How does it feel?
   a) Smooth.
   b) Brittle.

10 Ask someone who doesn't know to guess how old you are. Are they:
   a) Close (give or take two years either side of your real age)?
   b) Wide of the mark?

Your score:

If you scored mostly a) – you're doing some things right, which will have helped to counteract the damaging effects of smoking.

If you scored mostly b) – you're not helping yourself. Now that you've stopped smoking, learn to maximise your good looks!

'Do not regret growing older. It is a privilege denied to many.'
Unknown

Activity

How do I look?

Stand in front of a mirror, in good light. Take a long hard look at your face. What would you like to improve? You don't have to do anything drastic, but a few changes could help boost your confidence as a non-smoker. Giving up is all about feeling good, after all.

Men – how about shaving off that beard or using moisturiser?

Women – why not book a facial now that your skin has a chance to reap the benefits?

STAYING STOPPED

81

> **Did you know?**
>
> In 1985 the term 'Smoker's Face' was added to the medical dictionary. The characteristics of Smoker's Face, which tends to make people look older than they are, were defined as follows:
>
> Lines or wrinkles on the face, particularly radiating at right angles from the upper and lower lips or corners of the eyes, deep lines on the cheeks or numerous shallow lines on the cheeks and lower jaw.

How smoking ages you

- Along with sun damage and hard living, nicotine can add years to your appearance.
- The effects of smoking in terms of ageing are significant.
- Inhaling one puff of cigarette smoke produces a trillion free radicals* in the lungs.
- The free radicals are transported around the body, causing untold damage to cells.
  *Free radicals are aggressive chemicals that cause harm in the body.

TOP TIP

- Anti-oxidants are the good guys that combat free-radicals. Boost your anti-oxidant intake by eating lots of beans, fruits and veg – especially berry fruits and tomatoes.

The effects of smoking on skin

- Smoking leads to poor circulation, which stops the flow of essential nutrients reaching the skin.
- Skin can appear dull and grey as a result.
- Smokers' features often have a gaunt and bony look.
- Smoking causes wrinkles, especially around the eyes and mouth.
- Nicotine turns your fingertips brown or yellow.

Skin cancer risk

The number of cigarettes you smoke each day is directly linked to your chances of developing skin cancer.

No. of cigarettes smoked daily	Increase in risk of skin cancer
1–10	x 2.4
1–20	x 3.3
20+	x 4

Activity
Look after your skin

Follow a skin-care plan and see the difference.

Know your skin type – and choose skin products accordingly

1 Dry (prone to flakiness and a dull complexion).

2 Oily (shiny texture with open pores and prone to blemishes).

3 Combination (a mixture of the above).

Cleanse, tone and moisturise, morning and night

1 Cleansing stops dirt, sweat, make-up and bacteria blocking your pores and causing blemishes.

2 Toning removes excess cleanser and tightens up your pores.

3 Moisturising ensures your skin is nourished and doesn't dry out.

Exfoliate

Use a gentle exfoliator every week to slough away dead skins cells and help your pores breathe.

STAYING STOPPED

You've been a non-smoker for a whole month. That's brilliant! Today is a day for feeling extra-positive about what you've achieved. With so many non-smoking days behind you, you can really begin to feel like a non-smoker. It's important to feel this on the inside, but the outside matters too. It's time to take a look at how much better you'll look now that you're fag free.

The effect of smoking on hair

◆ Smoking can cause dull, lank and smelly hair.
◆ Smoking stops nutrients reaching the hair so it can struggle to stay healthy.
◆ Long hair in particular becomes brittle and can break.
◆ Giving up means you can have shiny, healthy hair.
◆ What's more, the money you save on cigarettes will pay for you to have good haircuts, experiment with colour and try different styles.

Did you know?

Hair grows about 12 mm per month.

A single strand lives for up to seven years.

If you never cut your hair, it would grown to a length of 107 cm before falling out.

There are 120,000 hairs on the average adult head.

Blondes have the most at 14,000.

Redheads have the least at 90,000.

Women tend to lose about 20 per cent of their hair between the ages of 40 and 50. Smoking can accelerate this.

Hair grows faster in the summer, while you're asleep and between the ages of 16 and 24.

Hair is slightly elastic and can stretch by 20–30 per cent before snapping.

A human hair is stronger than a copper wire of the same thickness.

The combined strength of a head of human hair could support the weight of 99 people.

In 1703, Peter the Great of Russia created a tax on beards that almost caused a revolution.

Hair dos… (and hair don'ts!)

DO

- Choose the right shampoo for your type of hair.
- Use an intensive treatment once a week for six weeks after you stop smoking.
- Let your hair air-dry as often as possible.
- Use a comb rather than a brush on long hair.
- Shampoo, condition and rinse extra well after swimming.

DON'T

- Be surprised if your favourite shampoo loses its touch. Hair is affected by changes in the environment. Change shampoo type every so often.
- Be rough when drying your hair with a towel. You'll damage it.
- Overuse hot blow-dryers, crimpers and tongs.

Activity Care for your hair

Your hair has a chance to shine now that it's smoke free. Look after it!

Book an appointment with a good hairdresser and talk through the best look for you.

CHECK ✔

This week I have:
- re-read Days 14–16 to remind myself how to cope with cravings and side effects.

Before I go out (looking great!) I will read through the socialising action plan on Day 34.

STAYING STOPPED

What you wear reflects your personality – and you're a smart, courageous person who's triumphed over giving up smoking. It's time for a wardrobe makeover!

Activity

Get a Life! style quiz

1 When you get dressed in the morning, what goes through your mind?
a) I wore this yesterday, but I think I can get away with it again today.
b) All these clothes and nothing to wear!
c) I love this hand-me-down jacket – it's been in the family for years.

2 What do you see when you look in a full-length mirror?
a) A Hollywood beauty.
b) I don't have a full-length mirror.
c) Everything I don't want to be.

3 How do you want to feel when you get dressed?
a) Sexy.
b) Comfortable.
c) Invisible.

4 How much do you enjoy shopping for clothes?
a) I love it.
b) It's something practical I have to do, like food shopping.
c) I hate it.

5 What type of clothes suit your everyday lifestyle?
a) Smart casual – I can wear anything within reason.
b) Formal – I have to wear a suit every day.
c) I don't feel I have a daily identity.

6 If someone compliments your outfit do you...?
a) Say thank you, and leave it at that.
b) Brush away the compliment with a self-deprecating comment.
c) Think they are lying.

Your score

Give yourself for every: a) 2 points; b) 1 point;
c) 0 points.

5 or more points: You enjoy clothes and know
what makes you look and feel good. You have a
style that works for you. You can enjoy clothes
even more as a non-smoker.

Under 5 points: You need to feel more confident
with clothes and build a wardrobe that suits your
lifestyle. Remember, the latest high street fashion
is less important than choosing outfits that fit you
well and show off your best points. And yes, you
do have good points, whatever your shape! Use
your new found self-confidence as an ex-smoker
to brush up your fashion sense.

'We really aren't interested in following trends. We want people to
wear what suits them. People can become more confident almost
immediately by the clothes they wear.' Trinny Woodall and
Susannah Constantine of *What Not to Wear*, BBC TV

Did you know?

Smokers are twice as likely as non-smokers to lose their sight, according
to recent research by the Royal National Institute for the Blind.

STAYING STOPPED

What is style?

Style is quite simply wearing what suits us – it's not about designer labels and expensive shoes. Anyone can learn to dress well – and there's no better time than now to brush up your image as a new non-smoker. Style is about confidence and making the most of what you have. You don't need to look like a model to feel good about how you look. Achieving non-smoker status will give you bags of confidence. Capitalise on it with a few well-chosen items to improve your wardrobe.

Fashion tips for women

1 Wear what suits you. Go shopping with a friend and ask them to be honest about what looks good. The latest trends might look great on the catwalk – but how do they look on you?
2 Less is more when it comes to fashion. A few quality classics that you can dress up will work better than dozens of cheaper outfits.
3 Shop in advance for a special occasion. If you try to find your perfect outfit on the day that you need it, you'll just end up stressed.
4 Feel comfortable in what you wear. The strapless dress may look great in the shop, but constantly checking if it's staying up will ruin the image.
5 Don't underestimate the importance of underwear. A good bra is essential to show off your figure to its best advantage. Get measured.
6 Don't be tempted to over accessorise. Jewellery should enhance an outfit, not dominate it.

Fashion tips for men

1 Leave your comedy clothes in the wardrobe. T-shirts with slogans and cartoon-character ties are naff.
2 Define your own style. Smart casual is acceptable almost anywhere now. If you're not sure of the dress code for a restaurant or party – ask in advance.

STAYING STOPPED

3 Smart separates are fine, but there's no need to look scruffy. Jeans look great paired with a crisp white shirt. Polo necks are good under a jacket.

4 Don't let shopping become a chore if you're not interested in clothes. Make a list of what you need a few times a year and set aside an afternoon to go shopping.

5 Don't rely on girlfriends, wives or mothers to shop for you. You need to try things on to ensure a good fit.

6 Make sure your outfits are washed and ironed.

Activity

Whose style do you admire?

- Think of someone famous whose style you admire. This person must be a non-smoker.

- Write down three items that you could add to your wardrobe that would give you a hint of their style.

1 ....

2 ....

3 ....

TOP TIP

- Remind your body you're a non-smoker. Breathe deeply and feel your lungs filling up with fresh air.

STAYING STOPPED

Spend an afternoon dressing up. Make sure you have at least an hour free to go through everything in your wardrobe. Try everything on and after having a good look in the mirror, decide what stays and what goes.

Activity

Sort out your wardrobe

- Clear out your wardrobe and pile everything on the bed.

- Clean the inside of your wardrobe.

- Chuck out any mis-shapen hangers and invest in some new ones.

Wardrobe or charity shop?

Ask yourself these questions if you can't decide which pile to put something on:

1 If you were trying this item on in a shop, would you still buy it now?
   a) Yes – wardrobe.
   b) No – charity shop.
2 How do you feel the moment you put this item on?
   a) Uplifted – you love it! Wardrobe.
   b) Unsure – you have to stare in the mirror for ages to make up your mind. Charity shop.
3 Are you hanging on to this item for sentimental reasons?
   a) Yes – charity shop.
   b) No – wardrobe.
4 How would you feel if you bumped into someone you wanted to impress while wearing this item?
   Smart and confident – wardrobe.
   Embarrassed – charity shop.

5 Has the item lost its shape or lustre, however much you like it?
Yes – charity chop.
New – wardrobe.

◆ Hang up the items you're keeping carefully.
◆ Ensure that there's space between hangers and nothing is crumpled.
◆ Save space by folding jeans and jumpers that won't crease.
◆ Pair matching outfits together.
◆ Make a list of any essentials you need to buy.
◆ Look forward to spending some of the money you've saved from not smoking on some new additions to your wardrobe.

The effect of smoking on clothes

Clothes trap smoke, which is why they smell so bad the morning after a night on the town. The more you wash your clothes, the more quickly the fibres will wear out and they'll lose their shape. Smokers have higher dry cleaning bills than non-smokers!

 TOP TIP

● Don't be afraid to clear out clothes and accessories that you've had forever! It's all part of stepping out of the old life, into the new.

Tactical thinking

Research shows that young male smokers are less concerned about the effect of cigarettes on their health than they are about how they look and how they appeal to the opposite sex. In response, the Department of Health ran this poster campaign in men's pub toilets:

Bad news. Smoking causes impotence.

More bad news. These ads are in the ladies too!

STAYING STOPPED

It's fun to think of the ways your life will improve as a non-smoker. But although you've come a long way – you're not out of the woods yet. It's important to keep building on the practical skills you've been learning as you go along.

Danger zone checklist

Are you doing any of the following?

◆ Inhaling smoke from other people's cigarettes.
◆ Lighting friends' fags for them.
◆ Having a quick puff on a fag or cigar at the end of a meal, even if you don't inhale.
◆ Holding an unlit cigarette in your hands, just to see how it feels.
◆ Smoking herbal cigarettes that don't contain nicotine.
◆ Smoking a joint.

If you tick any of the above, you're on a slippery slope to starting to smoke again. Stop. Treat it as a wake-up call. Read through your no-smoking notebook and go back through the pages of this book to reinforce everything you've learned.

Visualisation techniques

These are mind exercises that help to achieve a particular goal – similar to those that are used in yoga and meditation. Visualisation uses mental images to inspire particular feelings – your reasons not to smoke in this case.

Example:

Josie is giving up smoking because she wants to get fit. She paints a mental picture of herself crossing the finish line in a half-marathon. Josie then needs to 'colour-in' the picture. She takes a big gulp of air and imagines how she'll feel as the crowds are cheering and she's heading towards the tape.

Activity

Create a visualisation technique

Create a visualisation technique of your own. Write it down using the same steps in the example. Here are a few suggestions to get you going:

1 Picture the freedom of not being controlled by cigarettes. Imagine strolling along a beautiful, white, sandy beach, with the waves lapping at your feet. How do you feel in this picture?

2 Picture enjoying a meal in a restaurant you like. Imagine browsing through the dessert menu without even thinking of lighting a cigarette. What dessert will you choose? How will it taste?

3 Picture playing in the garden with your kids. Imagine keeping up with them and not feeling out of breath. Imagine giving them a clean, fresh kiss and snuggling them in your clean, fresh clothes.

You can devise as many visualisation techniques as you like – and call on them when the going gets tough.

- ◆ Strong, positive images will help you cope with cravings.
- ◆ They'll distract you and boost your willpower.
- ◆ The images you choose must focus on the good reasons for quitting.
- ◆ They should be pleasant, fulfilling and relaxing images to help reduce stress – one of the things that can trigger a relapse.

STAYING STOPPED

A word about quitting together

Plenty of people find themselves a partner or 'buddy' who gives up smoking at the same time as they do. This can be a great idea, especially in the early days when you really need someone to understand how you're feeling. But around about now, when you're over the worst but giving up still feels like a grind, cracks can appear in this system. If your partner or a member of your group starts smoking again, it's important not to let yourself be influenced by their decision.

- *Don't* see it as a sign that giving up is far too hard.
- *Don't* listen if they try to convince you they're pleased they started smoking again.
- *Do* seek support elsewhere.
- *Do* remember that if you start smoking again now, you'll have to go through all this again in the future.

> Remember – quitting smoking is now an NHS priority area, so clinics and other services to support smokers are being set up around the country. Even if there's no formal clinic in your area, you can still get advice from pharmacists, doctors and practice nurses.

No more excuses!

⑧ I smoke because it helps me to concentrate.

Long after they've given up, smokers will often feel tempted to reach for a cigarette when they need to focus their minds. But inhaling nicotine doesn't in fact help. Blood nicotine levels fluctuate wildly in smokers. Depending on how many you smoke a day, there will come a point between cigarettes when all you can think of is when you can have the next one, making it difficult to concentrate on any other task.

Non-smokers can sustain their levels of concentration. Smokers have erratic concentration levels.

STAYING STOPPED

Another good reason to give up (as if you needed one!)

- Every three days, someone dies because of a cigarette fire.
- Fires started by cigarettes are the most fatal – often because the smoker is asleep when the fire takes hold.
- Six out of ten of those killed in cigarette fires are men.
- 17 per cent of smokers confess to smoking in bed.
- Nearly half of all households have a smoker living in them.
- Smoking households are nearly one and a half times more likely to have a fire than non-smoking homes.

Activity

Beat the clock

- See how quickly you can write a list of ten good reasons to give up smoking. Your target is 30 seconds.

- Keep practising until you can hit the target. Writing the list will make sure the good reasons for giving up are always at the top of your mind.

STAYING STOPPED

In this chapter, the programme has looked at how you need to build a new image of yourself in your mind. Once you think of yourself as a non-smoker, you'll believe you are a non-smoker – and that's the way you'll stay. If you've made it this far without a cigarette you've done fantastically well. If you've had the odd relapse but are still on track, you're doing well too. It's always better to keep trying than to give up giving up. Remember – Day 26 is the day you need to refer back to if you do slip up.

So, you've had a careful look at the clothes you wear and the image you'd like to project. You've learned how to make the most of your new shiny, smoke-free hair and your healthy, rosy skin! To top things off, what you need is a nice, bright smile.

Smoking and your teeth

Smoking has the following effect on teeth and gums. Be honest. How many of the signs can you already see?

1 Staining. The nicotine and tar in cigarettes stains teeth yellow, brown, dark brown and, in some cases, black. Not a pretty sight.
Are your teeth stained?
2 Gum disease. Smoking causes gum disease.
Do your gums look red and squashy where they join the teeth?
(They should be firm, and light pink.)
3 Smokers are more likely to lose their teeth earlier than non-smokers.
Are any of your teeth wobbly?

How many did you answer 'yes' to? Even if it was only one or two, now is a good time to book a dental appointment.

Activity

Visiting the dentist

If you haven't been to the dentist for a long time ask a friend or colleague to recommend one. Many dentists take private patients only these days, but the money you're saving on cigarettes will easily cover the cost of a twice-yearly appointment.

If you're going for a regular check up, make sure you tell your dentist you have stopped smoking. Get them to tell you the positive effects this will have on your oral health. The dentist will be only too pleased to encourage you!

Did you know?

When you smoke, the cigarette smoke you inhale condenses and about 70 per cent of the tar contained in the smoke is deposited in the lungs.

Mouth cancer

More young people are getting mouth cancer according to a 2005 report by the British Dental Health Foundation. Previously, older men were most at risk, but now it seems smoking and binge drinking are changing the trend. The disease affects 4,300 people in Britain each year in the UK. 1,700 people die as a result. The first sign is often a mouth ulcer that fails to heal. Ask your dentist if you're concerned.

STAYING STOPPED

Going to the dentist is a bit like having a cleaner coming to clean your house. You have to tidy up first!

Activity

Give your mouth an MOT

- Floss between your teeth, making sure you reach right into the back of your mouth.

- Brush your teeth thoroughly for at least three minutes.

- Don't just concentrate on the front teeth – get the toothbrush around the back of those molars!

- Freshen up your breath by gargling with a mouthwash. (If you're eating healthily and not smoking, you shouldn't need to use a mouthwash every day.)

  This activity is not a one off – set aside an extra five minutes every evening for dental hygiene.

Now – open wide and look carefully at the inside of your mouth in the mirror.

What to look for

- If your gums bleed when you floss or brush, it could indicate the early signs of gum disease. Make sure you tell your dentist where this occurs.

- Pay extra attention to these areas. Regular flossing and brushing will ensure that no bits of food remain stuck between your teeth.

- If your teeth are stained, ask a chemist to recommend a good whitening toothpaste.

- Your dentist will be able to give you information about tooth-whitening procedures at the surgery.

TOP TIP

- Buy a new toothbrush today. Ask at the counter of a good chemist if you're not sure which is the best style for you.

Dare you try the breath test?

One of the most unpleasant side-effects of smoking is bad breath. You haven't smoked for a long time now, so the stale smoky smell should have left your mouth. But you want to be confident that your breath as a non-smoker is OK.

- After you've cleaned your teeth, ask your partner, relative or friend for an honest opinion.
- Exhale a quick puff of air, close up to them, and ask them to check your breath smells fresh.

If it does, great – another reason to feel pleased with your progress so far. If it doesn't, don't feel offended. It's far better that someone close tells you. Knowing about it means you can take action. Make a list of things you want to ask the dentist – and put 'fresh breath!' at the top.

What the dentist sees

- Smokers' mouths look older than the mouths of non-smokers.
- A smoker's mouth shows permanent tooth stain.
- Smokers' have thicker gums, where gum tissue has pulled away from the teeth.
- Smokers' tongues are darker in colour and coated in most cases.
- Smokers' teeth show wear on the biting surfaces.
- Smoking dries out the mouth, which is why smokers are more prone to halitosis or bad breath.

SMILE! None of the above need trouble you any more!

STAYING STOPPED

Your notes

CHAPTER 4

SMOKER PROFILES

People begin smoking for all kinds of different reasons.

ᴀᴄᴛⁱᵛⁱᵗʸ Activity

Are you living in the past?

The aim of this exercise is to get you thinking how far you've moved on from the days when you thought it might be fun or exciting to smoke cigarettes.

Take a trip back into the past. Take the following steps:

1   In your notebook, write a paragraph describing the first cigarette you smoked.

Write down:

1   the circumstances

2   who you were with

3   how you felt as you prepared to smoke your first cigarette

4   how you felt as you smoked it

5   how you felt after you'd smoked it.

If you can't remember the details, try to imagine how you felt and write down your thoughts.

2   Take a few minutes to read through your reasons.

3 Now, circle any of the following words that you've used.

Excited   Big   Peer pressure   Proud

Clever   Grown up   Rebellious

Do they seem relevant to your life as a smoker today?

If you answered 'no'...

Give yourself a pat on the back. You're not stuck in the past. You're moving forwards, well on the way to becoming a non-smoker.

If you answered 'yes'...

You're stuck in the past. If any of the words in '3' describe how you feel as an adult smoker, you need to ask yourself why – and realise how mistaken you are.

What's your profile?

You may have begun smoking with friends and you may have felt proud that you'd smoked your first fag. Cigarettes *are* highly addictive, but other factors have been at work too. Everyone is different, but most smokers can relate to one of the following categories of smoker. Don't worry if you don't fully understand the meaning of each category at this stage. Tick the category that you think describes you best:

◆ hardcore addict
◆ social smoker
◆ nervous smoker
◆ rebellious smoker
◆ guilty smoker
◆ always quitting smoker.

In this chapter, we'll be looking at the profiles and developing skills that can be used to your advantage – whatever type of smoker you are.

SMOKER PROFILES

Smoker profile 1 – the hardcore addict

The hardcore addict:

◆ began smoking at an early age
◆ smokes 20+ each day
◆ smokes their first cigarette within half an hour of waking up
◆ suffers mood change (irritability or anxiety) when deprived of nicotine
◆ avoids going to places where smoking is banned (e.g. flying, going to the cinema)
◆ feels that smoking is key to his or her identity
◆ has a cigarette last thing at night.

If you identify with five or more of the above, consider your smoker profile that of a hardcore addict.

Quitters' quips – profile

I'm 52 and I've smoked 30 cigarettes a day since I was 13. I had a heart operation last year, linked to my smoking, but I had a cigarette again a few days after the surgery. I think about smoking constantly. I don't sleep well and if I wake up in the middle of the night, I have a cup of tea and a cigarette. I am desperate to give up. Wanting to stop has taken over my life. I think about it all the time and when I smoke, I don't enjoy my cigarettes. I hate them and I hate myself for smoking them. I have tried to give up by willpower, but I have rarely got through a day without a cigarette. I haven't tried NRT – I feel I should be strong enough to give up on my own. – Ron

Advice
● Smokers often suffer low self-esteem and Ron may be in this category.
● He sets unrealistic and unnecessary goals.
● He beats himself up for not being able to give up, which is pointless.
● Why try to give up alone when there is so much help at hand?

SMOKER PROFILES

Action
- Don't be a martyr.
- Ask your GP or pharmacist about NRT.

There's no reason why you can't give up smoking if you are in this category, but it is crucial that you're prepared to let go of the image you have of yourself as a smoker. Thinking about your new image and believing that you'll enjoy being a non-smoker is your most important challenge.

Activity

Negatives and positives

Divide a page in two. Write ten words under each heading. The first column must consist of negative words only, and the second column of positive words only.

**Choker/
Negative words**

**Non-smoker/
Positive words**

- (e.g.) Smelly

- Fresh

....

....

TOP TIP

- If you're a hardcore addict, there is no reason why you can't be a hardcore non-smoker. Shift your focus. Think about the new you!

SMOKER PROFILES

Smoker profile 2 – the social smoker

The social smoker:

◆ began smoking in adolescence or adulthood
◆ always accepts a cigarette when offered
◆ sometimes goes all day without smoking
◆ always smokes in a social setting or when drinking alcohol
◆ thinks he or she 'enjoys' smoking
◆ is pleased to meet another smoker
◆ would feel awkward to be the only non-smoker in a group.

If you identify with five or more of the above, consider your smoker profile that of a social smoker. There's nothing positive about this category. Adding the word *social* to the definition might make you feel better, but you're kidding yourself. You are still a smoker, like any other.

Quitters' quips – profile

I'm a dancer, so I do need to be quite fit, but all the girls I work with smoke. I'm 30 and beginning to notice I'm out of breath at the end of my routine, much more than I've ever noticed before. I want to give up, but we spend a lot of time in smoking environments like clubs and at parties where we're performing. There's also a lot of hanging around, and having a smoke and a chat helps to pass the time. If I'm honest, I think if I gave up, I wouldn't feel like one of the gang any more, but I know that's not a very good reason to keep smoking. – Stacey

Advice

● Social smokers tend to worry about fitting in and Stacey is sensible enough to acknowledge this.
● She needs to boost her confidence and realise that her friends and colleagues like her for who she is, not because she smokes!

SMOKER PROFILES

Action

- Ask the girls what they think.
- Stacey will probably find one or two among them who'd like to give up too.
- Support each other.
- The biggest challenge for social smokers is that they let themselves off the hook. By thinking they just smoke to be sociable, they deny the fact that they are addicted as much as any one else.
- Face facts.

Activity
Make the most of yourself

- Look in the mirror. Smile!

- Think of all the things about your personality that you're proud of. Or get a friend to tell you what they like best about you.

- Smoking doesn't influence who likes you or how well you fit into a group.

- We all have some qualities we can make the most of.

TOP TIP

- Never be tempted to think, 'I'll just have the odd fag now and then.' Circumstances can change very quickly. Even if you manage it for a while, before you know it you'll be thinking about cigarettes every time you have a drink or every time you meet a friend who smokes.

SMOKER PROFILES

Smoker profile 3 – the nostalgic smoker

The nostalgic smoker:

- began smoking at a time of particular significance in their life
- associates cigarettes with this time (this may be a subconscious association)
- is reminded how they felt then, every time they smoke a cigarette
- thinks a cigarette makes them feel more content
- imagines smoking at certain events and looks forward to them for that reason
- feels better about themselves when holding a cigarette
- feels lost without cigarettes and misses smoking terribly.

If you identify with five or more of the above, consider your smoker profile that of a nostalgic smoker. The 'significant time' when you began smoking may have positive connotations (e.g. being young and free) or negative connotations (e.g. a bereavement). The connection that you make with smoking now and smoking in the past will often be subconscious, making it hard to identify.

Quitters' quips – profile

I had my first fag when I was in my early twenties. I left home and moved into a flatshare in Manchester with two friends. For the first time in our lives we were living by our own rules. We'd go out late and get drunk – or stay up, talking about life until the early hours of the morning. I loved those days – we had hardly a care in the world. Now I'm 38 with a job and a girlfriend and we have a baby girl. I don't want her to have a dad who smokes, but it's so hard to give up. – Garry

Advice

- Coupled with addiction, associating cigarettes with a particular time in our lives can be a strong link to break.
- It's important to think about the things in life you enjoy now. They may be different to the things you did in the past, but it doesn't mean they're not as good.
- Garry's baby daughter should give him a great motivation to stop.

Action

- Think hard about the time in your past that you most associate with smoking. Was it a positive time or a negative time?
- Put the past behind you and be determined to look forwards into the future.

⊚ TOP TIP

- Three out of four children know what cigarettes are by the time they're five years old. Children learn by imitation. Don't smoke around them.

'Throw caution to the wind and *just do it.*' Carrie Underwood

Activity
Associations with smoking

In your notebook write down five words that sum up the time in the past that you associate most with smoking. It doesn't matter if they're positive or negative words.

Now write down five words that sum up how you want your life to be as a non-smoker. These must be positive words.

SMOKER PROFILES

Smoker profile 4 – the rebellious smoker

The rebellious smoker:

◆ probably began smoking at school
◆ enjoys the fact that smoking is something people disapprove of
◆ thinks of smoking as a way of showing they won't conform
◆ still believes that smoking makes them look cool
◆ makes a point of being a smoker
◆ pretends not to care about smoking-related diseases
◆ feels slightly superior to be the smoker in a group.

If you identify with five or more of the above, consider your smoker profile that of a rebellious smoker. Well – how wrong can you be! Smoking may have given you an edge of cool among your classmates when you were 13 – but you're an adult now. How can you seriously believe, with all the medical knowledge available, that smoking is a smart thing to do?

Quitters' quips – profile

However much I get told smoking is bad for me, there's still something about it that makes me feel good. There is a stigma, but I don't care. I'm 45 and I work in an office. I like the fact that I can go outside and have a fag in the rain. It's time for myself, thinking time. Deep down I suppose I fear I might be a boring person without any vices. I never thought about getting ill until recently, when my cousin was diagnosed with lung cancer. We had our first cigarette together, decades ago. I know I have to give up and I'm trying hard. – Tariq

Advice
● Tariq says he doesn't care what people think, but often with rebellious smokers, there's a sense of bravado in their bold statements.
● Rebellious smokers often have a 'don't care' attitude, not because they mean it, but because they fear they won't be able to quit.

- If you're in this category you need to work very hard on being sure you want to give up.

Action

- Rebellious smokers need to feel different, which isn't a problem in itself. But find another, less destructive means of showing you're an individual.
- Your friends, colleagues and family will respect you for having the determination to stop smoking.
- You are the only one who thinks you're a sexy rebel.
- More people pity you than admire you. Is that how you want to be seen?

Activity

How do you feel?

Get to the root of the problem by answering these questions with absolute honesty. Nobody else needs to see the answers.

1 Imagine you're at a wedding or a party. You meet a new group of people who you like and admire. None of them smoke. When you say you're going outside for a fag, they laugh at you. How do you feel?

2 A close friend, also a committed smoker, has recently given up and says he feels great for doing it. How do you feel about his achievement?

3 When people talk about smoking-related diseases, you've always said 'When your number's up, it's up' or 'It'll never happen to me'. Your doctor has just diagnosed that you have lung cancer. How are you going to tell your friends, family and colleagues what's wrong with you?

SMOKER PROFILES

If you have stuck with the programme since your Quit Day, you have reached the six-week milestone. Congratulations!

Smoker profile 5 – the guilty smoker

The guilty smoker:

- is under pressure to give up from other people
- wishes everyone would get off their back
- lies about how many they smoke a day
- convinces themself they smoke less than they really do
- may keep the fact that they smoke from other people – even parents or partners
- would like to give up but finds it too much effort
- feels depressed that they can't give up.

If you identify with five or more of the above, consider your smoker profile that of a guilty smoker. Guilty smokers feel just that – guilty – every time they have a cigarette. Where's the pleasure in that? You don't even enjoy a fag – it makes you feel bad. Turn things around. Give up and have something to feel good about.

Quitters' quips – profile

When I got pregnant I gave up smoking, more or less for the whole nine months. I felt sick quite a lot so I didn't find it too hard. As soon as the baby was born, I wanted a cigarette. It's the first thing I thought of! Before I knew it I was smoking again – about ten a day – more if I go out for a drink. I hate the way people look at me in such a bad way if I'm having a fag while I'm pushing the buggy. I feel I'm a bad mother, but it's not their business to judge me. – Lara

Advice

- Guilty smokers, like many others, have low self-esteem.
- Lara should be enjoying being a new mum, but instead her time is taken up feeling bad about herself.
- This is an example of how cigarettes control and take over the lives of the people who smoke them.

Action

- Be determined to take control yourself.
- Focus on the new you and pay particular attention to your new image.
- Lara can paint a picture in her mind of how she wants to look as a smart, young mum.

Activity **Reality check**

- Stop being in denial.

- On a piece of paper, write the following phrase ten times.

  'I HAVE BEEN A SMOKER FOR .... YEARS.'

- Then turn the page over and write the following phrase 20 times.

  'I WILL SOON BE A NON-SMOKER.'

TOP TIP

- Whether you smoke one cigarette a week or 50 cigarettes a day, you are a smoker.

SMOKER PROFILES

Smoker profile 6 – the always quitting smoker

The always quitting smoker:

◆ knows they should give up but isn't sure they want to
◆ has tried to stop several times, but never managed for long
◆ doesn't change their life or routine when trying to give up
◆ doesn't seek help from their GP or pharmacist
◆ thinks a lot about giving up, but dreads having to do it
◆ thinks they will give up one day, just not yet
◆ feels depressed and miserable when not smoking.

If you identify with five or more of the above, consider your smoker profile that of an always quitting smoker. Always quitting smokers can never maximise their happiness in life because they're either feeling miserable that they are smoking, or miserable that they are not smoking. Again, low self-esteem is a problem. Plenty of people try to give up a few times before they are successful, but if this has been going on for years, you're bound to feel as though you're constantly failing.

Quitters' quips – profile

Over the last ten years I've tried to give up more times than I can remember. I've stopped dozens of times, but never for more than a few days. Sometimes I make quite a build up and tell lots of people I'm stopping for real, but the moment I go to the pub and have a drink, it's like my mind says, 'Oh have a fag, what's the point of being miserable.' So I have one. But I always wish I hadn't by the time I'm down to the stub. All this stopping and starting drives me crazy. If I could only say, 'I'm a non-smoker' and mean it, I'd be a happy man. – Jed

Advice
● Everyone will tell you that to stop for good, you really have to want to stop. That's why it's important to follow the steps in the programme that reinforce the positive benefits you will feel from not smoking.

Action

- Most of the time, you know that you don't want to be a smoker. It's only when you find yourself in particular social circumstances that you become convinced you want to smoke.
- You need to be prepared to avoid danger zones – such as the pub – for several weeks after your Quit Day.

Activity
Plan ahead

- The most important exercises in the 100-day programme for the always quitting smoker are those that encourage you to think positively about being a non-smoker – and distraction techniques.

- Learn to plan your socialising a week ahead and stick to the following criteria when you go out:
  1 Meet friends who don't smoke.
  2 Sit in no-smoking areas of bars and restaurants.
  3 Ask for their support.
  4 Go outside for a breath of fresh air if you crave a cigarette.
  5 Limit the time you spend in a social environment.
  6 Avoid alcohol – it will weaken your resolve.

TOP TIP

- Avoiding social occasions like going out for a drink might seem hard, but look at the overall context and timescale of your life. Even if you don't go out much during the whole of the 100-day programme, it'll be worth it in the long run.

SMOKER PROFILES

Smoker profile 7 – the nervous smoker

The nervous smoker:

- is convinced a cigarette is the best means of calming down
- feels that holding a cigarette keeps their hands busy
- feels more confident socially when holding a cigarette
- thinks other people will perceive them as more assertive if they smoke
- feels anxious in situations where they can't smoke
- feels anxious about the damaging effect of smoking on their health
- worries that non-smokers may look down at them.

If you identify with five or more of the above, consider your smoker profile that of a nervous smoker. If you began smoking during a stressful time in your life, you probably subconsciously connect having a cigarette with needing to feel calm, every time you light one. It's important that you pay particular attention to the early days of the programme, where you learned that inhaling nicotine is one of the worst things you can do to reduce overall stress levels.

Quitters' quips – profile

I didn't smoke until I was 30. My dad died suddenly, and while I was getting over the shock, I was offered whisky and cigarettes. I remember that time as a haze of smoke and the strong taste of whisky, and feeling very upset and stressed. It was ten years ago and now I can remember my dad with a smile and fond memories. I still feel sad that he's not around and always have a cigarette when I look at photographs of him or talk about him. But I smoke at other times too. Cigarettes feel like a security blanket – they help to get me through a hard time. – Lorraine

Advice
- Lorraine associates smoking with a sad time and now worries that she can't cope without cigarettes.

- But, over time, she has coped with her bereavement emotionally.
- She needs to be confident that her cigarettes are a crutch she doesn't need.

Action

- Remind yourself that smoking doesn't relieve stress, it creates a vicious circle that means you're never free of stress, because your body is always anxious for more nicotine.
- Develop more effective methods of relaxation – in particular, learn to breathe deeply when you feel anxious.

Activity Try doing nothing!

- Nervous smokers often say they don't know what to do with their hands without a cigarette to hold.

- Try doing nothing! Standing with a glass in one hand and simply letting your free hand rest by your side will make you look more at ease than if you're fussing with cigarettes and lighters. Practice – you'll soon get used to it.

Be confident!

Having an idea of your smoker profile will help you to focus on the particular challenges that may affect you as an individual as you make your way through the 100-day programme.

Activity

How are you feeling?

- Use the knowledge you have gained from reading the smoker profiles to assess your personal progress.

- Draw a line down the middle of the page in your notebook, and head each column like this:

Achievements   **Challenges**

- Make a list of your best achievements in the six weeks since your Quit Day.

- In the second column, note down what you still find difficult.

- Under column one you might write 'Not smoking at cousin's wedding'.

- Under column two you might write 'Miss smoking when I make a phone call'.

- Writing your achievements alongside what you still find hard will remind you how well you're doing, and warn you of the danger zones you need to look out for.

TOP TIP

- All the way through the 100-day programme, you must focus on what you're gaining, not what you're missing from not smoking.
- Think: more money – less risk of illness – no stigma – freedom!

Positive thinking

Our inner thoughts have a powerful effect on how we see ourselves and the world. Negative thoughts can become self-fulfilling prophecies, so if you feel yourself thinking, 'Giving up isn't worth it', you're more likely to fail. Negative thought patterns embed themselves over years and it can take a lot of work to retrain long-held assumptions. But it is possible. In fact, there's a whole type of therapy called behavioural therapy that's designed to help you do this.

An example

When a negative thought pops into your head, you need to get rid of it – quickly!

Learn to replace your negative thoughts immediately.

So, 'I'm still getting cravings, they'll never go away' becomes, 'The craving will pass. I'm going to distract myself until it does.'

No more excuses!

(9) I smoke because I'm bored.

Do you really want to be the sort of person who can't think of anything better to do than have a cigarette? If you're waiting for a train you might get a craving and think a fag might kill time, but it's not really because of boredom. At the first opportunity, your addicted brain is simply telling you, 'Have a fag – that's a good idea.' You're more imaginative than that!

'In order to succeed, your desire for success should be greater than your fear of failure.' Bill Cosby, actor

Keep talking

Don't let your first conversation about smoking with your doctor be your last. If you relapse make sure you tell them. Even if you're feeling embarrassed or depressed about it, it's good to be honest. And when you successfully kick the habit, share the news! It might be the best thing your doctor has heard all day.

SMOKER PROFILES

You might be in the middle of the 100-day programme, but you'll have noticed by now that life goes on around you. It would be nice if you could hibernate and wake up 43 days from now as a confirmed non-smoker, but it's not going to happen! Now that you're becoming more confident as a non-smoker, it's important to plan for unforeseen circumstances.

Activity

Coping with stress

- Nobody wants to think about a distressing event, but spend a few moments putting an action plan in place to cope if you find yourself in an unexpectedly stressful situation.

- If you're confronted with a difficult life event at home or at work, how will you ensure that you won't reach for a cigarette to help you through?

- Draw on what you've learned about yourself so far to devise an emergency plan that will work for you.

Smoking and bereavement

Even people who haven't had a cigarette for many years can find that a traumatic event in their life can trigger a need to smoke again. The death of a loved one is the most likely time for this to occur. It is understandable why this happens. Your mind is so consumed with distress that it seems as though nothing else matters. So why on earth should it matter to have a cigarette? This is why:

- Smoking will not make things better.
- Nicotine will interfere with the 'distress' chemicals your brain produces at this time.

- Your immune system is under a massive amount of pressure when you suffer a bereavement.
- Your resistance to viruses, infections and abnormal pre-cancerous cells is lower than usual.

Ten points to remember when coping with bereavement or extreme stress

1 Rest as much as you can.
2 Eat fresh, healthy food. Even if you have no appetite, you must keep your body fuelled.
3 Cut down on caffeine, sugar and alcohol.
4 Talk to friends, family or a counsellor about your feelings.
5 Ask them for extra support.
6 Don't be embarrassed to mention that you are worried that you may start smoking again.
7 It may seem trivial to worry about cigarettes now, but it's important to your long-term wellbeing.
8 Don't let your mind go down the route of 'What does it matter if I smoke now?'
9 Refuse if other people offer you cigarettes.
10 Remember that your own health will be at risk if you smoke under extreme stress.

'Refusing to ask for help when you need it is refusing someone the chance to be helpful.' Ric Ocasek, musician

⊙ TOP TIP

- Taking exams, losing or changing your job, or splitting up with a partner are just a few examples of life events that could tempt you to have a cigarette and undo all your hard work. Think 'I will not smoke' when *anything* stressful happens to you!

SMOKER PROFILES

As well as devising an emergency plan for an unexpected traumatic event, it's equally important that you have a plan in place to cope with joyful situations that could see you reaching for the fags before you know it.

During the 100-day programme you need to be on constant alert to ensure you don't relapse at an impromptu social occasion. But what about a big event? A wedding or a christening where you'll gather to celebrate with all your family and friends – some of whom you may not see very often?

TOP TIP

- Don't allow yourself to use the excuse, 'It's a one-off occasion, so I can bum a one-off smoke from a friend.' Before you know it, you'll have gone through a whole packet and undone all your hard work.

Petal power

In each of the petals, write a short note that will reinforce your motivation. The first one is written in for you!

'The difference between the impossible and the possible lies in a man's determination.'
Tommy Lasorda, baseball star

What to say when somebody offers you a cigarette

By now, most of your friends and colleagues will know how determined you are to give up smoking. If they're not encouraging, be very suspicious of their motives. Do they smoke themselves? Then don't forget they would rather you kept them company than successfully join the ranks of the non-smokers! At a family do, however, you may be getting back in contact with people who don't know how serious you are about quitting.

Don't be tempted to get into a long discussion about how and why you are giving up. Say no to the cigarette that's offered and move the conversation on to a more interesting topic. The most effective conversation will go like this:

Guest 1: 'Would you like a cigarette?'

Quitter: 'No thanks – I've given up. So, what were you saying about ...'

At this stage in the programme, you should be confident of your success. The more you say that you've given up, the more you will believe in yourself.

Activity

Have a relaxing bath

This is a great relaxation technique for when you come home from a big occasion. Do it today, so you know what you have to look forward to.

- Run a bath as hot as you like it.

- Relax and soak for a few minutes, no longer.

- Take out the plug and let about a quarter of the water out.

- Top up with cold water and notice the change in your body temperature.

- Repeat a few times.

SMOKER PROFILES

Throughout the programme we've concentrated on giving up cigarettes. But what about other forms of nicotine inhalation?

Warning!

If you're giving up cigarettes, don't be tempted to move onto cigars,
roll ups or smoking a joint. Inhaling the contents of any of these is
equally bad for you!

The difference between cigars and cigarettes

Cigarettes
+ Same size
+ Contain less than 1 gram
  tobacco
+ Take ten minutes to smoke
+ Nicotine content appx.
  8.4 mg

Cigars
+ Different sizes
+ Contain 5–17 grams tobacco
+ Take up to two hours to smoke
+ Nicotine content 100–450 mg

What's in a cigar?

+ Some cigars contain the tobacco equivalent of an entire pack of
  cigarettes.
+ A cigar is up to seven inches long.
+ Different types of tobacco are used in cigars.
+ Cigars go through a long ageing and fermentation process in which
  high concentrations of carcinogenic compounds are produced.
+ Cigar wrappers are less porous than cigarette wrappers.
+ Compared with cigarette smoke, the concentrations of toxins and
  irritants are higher in cigar smoke.

Scientific evidence has shown that cancers of the oral cavity (lip, tongue, mouth and throat), larynx, lung and oesophagus are particularly associated with cigar smoking. Evidence strongly suggests a link between cigar smoking and cancer of the pancreas. Daily cigar smokers are at increased risk from developing heart and lung disease.

'But I don't inhale when I smoke a cigar!' This doesn't mean you're less at risk.

- Your lips, mouth, tongue, throat and larynx are directly exposed to smoke and its harmful carcinogens.
- Even holding an *unlit* cigar between the lips exposes these areas to carcinogens.
- When saliva containing smoke constituents is swallowed, the oesophagus is exposed to carcinogens.

Activity
Go outside and breathe!

- Make a point of going outside today, just to breathe fresh air. If you can, go for a walk. Stop for five minutes and spend the time inhaling deeply, pulling the air as far down into your lungs as you can.

- Think! Your lungs are clean now.

- Imagine! What would they look like if you were still smoking. Be pleased you are more than halfway towards your goal of going from choker to non-smoker.

SMOKER PROFILES

Are you still thinking positively? Let's check ...

The following three common negative thoughts have been turned into positive thoughts.

Negative	Positive
1 My bum looks big in this.	I look and feel great.
2 I don't think xxx likes me.	I have plenty of friends.
3 I handled that meeting badly.	I am competent in meetings.

Now think of three more negative thoughts that are personal to you, and give them the same treatment.

Negative	Positive
1	....
2	....
3	....

Put that in your pipe and smoke it!

Most people think smoking a pipe is less harmful than smoking cigarettes or cigars. But when you decide to give up smoking, you do exactly that, *give up smoking*. There are no substitutes and no alternatives. So if you're giving up – the pipe has to go too.

Doctors from the American Cancer Society found that smoking a pipe increased the risk of six cancers, namely cancer of the colon, oesophagus, larynx, lung, oropharynx and pancreas. It also increased the risk of heart disease, stroke and chronic lung disease. The doctors said that while smoking a pipe is not as dangerous as smoking cigarettes, it can still seriously damage health: 'All tobacco products cause excessive morbidity and mortality.'

Dream diary

Lots of people who have given up smoking continue to have dreams about smoking for a long while after they have stopped. Don't worry if this is happening to you – it doesn't mean you want to begin again, just that your body and mind is still adjusting to the big changes you're making.

Activity
Keep a dream diary

- Keep a dream diary for a week in your notebook.
- Jot down any dreams you remember as soon as you wake up.
- At the end of the week, look to see how many of them involved cigarettes.
- In the dreams, was smoking making you happy or unhappy?
- Most people who have smoking dreams once they've stopped are pleased to wake up and remember they don't smoke anymore!

No more excuses!

10 **I smoke because I don't care about the health risks.**

If you truly feel this, you may be suffering from depression, which can be aggravated by cigarettes, cigars, pipe smoking or cannabis smoking. By deliberately doing something that you know is bad for you, you are lowering your self-esteem. This creates a vicious circle:

- ◆ you feel miserable so you have a smoke …
- ◆ having a smoke makes you feel miserable … and so on.

When people do manage to stop smoking, they feel fantastically proud of what they've achieved. Remember – we're making a new you. When you've reached your goal, you'll have a far more positive outlook on life.

'You are never too old to set another goal or to dream a new dream.' C. S. Lewis, author

SMOKER PROFILES

So you've stubbed out the cigarettes and cigars – and put down the pipe. If you ever smoke cannabis, that has to stop too, if you're serious about becoming a non-smoker. Around 3.2 million people in the UK smoke cannabis, making it one of the most readily obtainable recreational drugs in Britain. There's a lot of debate about the effects it has on mental health. But because it's such a political topic, the health risks of inhaling a joint are often overlooked.

What we do know is this:

1 Most people who stop smoking cannabis (which is, of course, an illegal drug) continue to smoke, or take up smoking, cigarettes.
2 You are more likely to fail in giving up cigarettes if you continue to smoke cannabis.
3 Smoking three cannabis cigarettes a day is as dangerous as having a whole packet of standard cigarettes, according to the British Lung Foundation (BLF).
4 Regular smokers of cannabis are at increased risk of developing the potentially fatal lung disease emphysema.

What is emphysema?

Emphysema is a form of lung disease. Like chronic bronchitis, it generally occurs as a result of smoking, which damages the elastic supporting structure within the lungs. This leads to breakdown and collapse of some of the airways, which causes air to become trapped and the lungs over-inflated. Long-term heavy smokers may get emphysema and bronchitis together.

Cannabis risks

- Deeper inhalation causes more damage to lungs.
- Hand-rolled joints have no filter – meaning four times more nicotine is inhaled – that's just the *nicotine*, not the cannabis.
- Smoking cannabis and tobacco together is dramatically worse than smoking each separately, according to a BLF report.
- Tar from cannabis cigarettes contains 50 per cent more cancer causing carcinogens than tobacco.

Activity

Smoking associations

It may be a harsh realisation to some people that 'no smoking' means no smoking ... *anything*.

- Think of as many items as you can that you associate with smoking. Examples might include ashtrays, cigarette papers, pipes and matches.

- Imagine gathering them all together into a pile.

- Now, imagine throwing them all into a bottomless pit.

- Picture each item falling, falling, far beyond your reach.

SMOKER PROFILES

Your notes

....

....

....

....

....

....

....

....

....

....

....

....

....

....

....

CHAPTER 5

HEALTH BENEFITS

By now, you are well on your way to becoming an ex-smoker. You may still think about cigarettes, and you'll probably experience cravings every so often. But if you think back to the early days – NS +1 to QD +20 – your life without cigarettes should have become more manageable on a day-to-day basis.

> 'Don't give up at half time. Concentrate on winning the second half.' Paul Bryant, American football coach

Keep reminding yourself why you've given up

Stopping smoking can make you feel miserable in the short term. If you don't feel strongly motivated, it will be harder to resist cravings. Smokers need to be very clear about their reasons for giving up, and motivation should be clear and personal. In other words, we need to know why we're putting ourselves through something very difficult.

Checklist – true or false?

Answer true or false to the following five statements:

1 I think about cigarettes less often than I did when I first gave up.
2 It is getting easier to be a non-smoker.
3 Sometimes, I realise I haven't missed having a cigarette for hours at a time.
4 I am enjoying being a non-smoker.
5 I am confident I will see the 100-day programme through to the end.

Ideally, you'll have answered 'true' to all the statements. Don't worry if one or two were 'false' – but if three plus of your answers were 'false', it's worth seeking extra support.

- Ask your GP for advice.
- Join a stop-smoking clinic in your area.
- Investigate alternative stop-smoking methods such as hypnotherapy or acupuncture.

Phasing out NRTs

Around this time, you need to begin phasing out any smoking substitutes that have helped you up until now. Prepare yourself psychologically for this in the same way as you prepared for your Quit Day at the beginning of the programme. It's time to move on to the next stage of the process – where you simply don't think about cigarettes. You won't be able to do this if you are still using patches or chewing gum. It's OK to cut down on NRTs gradually – but try to wean yourself off them altogether in under two weeks. Any longer will only delay the time it takes for you to be completely free.

Activity

Visualise the end

Remember to put the visualisation techniques you learned into regular practice. (You can find them on Day 44.) For today's task:

- Imagine waking up one morning with absolutely no desire to smoke.

- You're a non-smoker who has survived the struggle.

- You are free from your addiction and happy you gave up smoking.

- How do you feel? How would life be different?

HEALTH BENEFITS

It's important to keep reminding yourself of the benefits you'll experience as a non-smoker, especially as you may be in the process of weaning yourself off NRTs. The purpose of the 100-day programme is not to bully you into quitting, but to *motivate* you into quitting. Remember:

◆ Only you have the final say in the matter of whether you smoke again or not.
◆ Nobody can do it for you.
◆ It's your responsibility.

In the early days of the programme, exposure to horror stories of smoking-related diseases may have seemed so daunting that you'd be put off even trying to give up! But now that you've come so far and not smoked for so long, learning about the nasty effects of smoking can boost your morale. After all, with every day that passes (and it's 51 so far!) you are lowering your risk of getting cancers, heart and lung disease. You've worked hard at discovering what motivated you to smoke, which isn't always easy to fathom. The cold, bare facts about the health risks of tobacco are much more stark.

Activity
Starting from scratch

Spend a few moments today imagining what it would be like to have to begin the 100-day programme all over again. Remember to call on that thought if you feel you might relapse. Having come so far, the thought of going back to NS+1 should be enough to put you off.

HEALTH BENEFITS

Interpreting facts

When confronted with the truth about the devastating effect that smoking has on the body, smokers and non-smokers react in different ways. Compare the differences in the lists below and feel proud and grateful that you can now put yourself in the first category.

Look at the common statement: *Smoking kills*. It's an image we see every day. How do you react to it?

Non-smokers

◆ Don't have to worry!
◆ Have no barriers to feeling fit and healthy.
◆ Feel good that the statement doesn't affect them.

Smokers

◆ Feel bombarded with negative publicity.
◆ Have niggling doubts about health.
◆ Feel their low self-esteem get lower.

Smoking does kill

The truth is that the evidence that smoking kills is overwhelming. There will always be exceptions to the rule, but it's highly unlikely that if you keep smoking, you'll live in good health to a ripe old age. Smoking doesn't just cut life expectancy, it causes damage to *every* organ and part of the body – inside and out, as we'll be finding out in this chapter.

We all know that smoking causes lung cancer. But had you thought about the reality of contracting the disease yourself? Very few lung cancer cases are diagnosed in young people, so smokers often find it easy to dismiss the reality of getting it.

Activity

What would life be like without your health?

Your risk of lung cancer is already decreasing – and has been since NS +1. But look at the list of symptoms below:

- Persistent cough
- Deep, wheezing cough
- Coughing up mucus
- Coughing up bloody sputum
- Recurring pneumonia or bronchitis
- Difficulty breathing
- Difficulty swallowing
- Permanent fatigue
- Loss of appetite.

Not nice are they?

- Visualise each symptom individually.
- Imagine yourself in the future, telling your doctor that you have these symptoms.
- How will you feel, knowing you could have avoided them?

By giving up now, you can stay fit and healthy. But next time you crave a cigarette, use this visualisation exercise to put you off having one (if you do recognise the symptoms in yourself, see a doctor).

HEALTH BENEFITS

Five facts about lung cancer

1 Lung cancer is one of the most dangerous cancers.
2 Four out of five lung cancer patients die within one year of being diagnosed.
3 More than 80 per cent of lung cancers are caused by smoking tobacco or by indirect exposure to tobacco smoke.
4 Some lung cancers do not cause any noticeable symptoms until they're advanced – and have spread to other parts of the body.
5 Stopping smoking instantly lowers your risk.

Other types of cancers linked to smoking	
Cervical cancer	Cancers of the mouth,
Cancer of the pancreas	Lip and throat
Cancer of the kidney	Bladder cancer
Liver cancer	Stomach cancer
	Leukaemia

Cancer treatments

Treatments for cancer include surgery, drugs, chemotherapy and radiotherapy. The drug treatments cause bruising, fatigue, hair loss, diarrhoea, nausea and vomiting.

Did you know?

Tobacco use kills around 106,000 people in the UK every year – that's more than 300 every day. It's the equivalent of a plane crashing every day. About half of all regular cigarette smokers will eventually be killed by their habit. Don't be one of them.

HEALTH BENEFITS

Heart disease is another big health risk associated with smoking. One in four of all smoking-related deaths in the UK is due to heart disease. Smokers are twice as likely as non-smokers to have a heart attack.

What is heart disease?

+ The heart needs a steady supply of blood to function effectively.
+ Smoking causes fatty deposits to build up in the arteries that carry blood into the heart.
+ This restricts the amount of blood that reaches the heart.
+ A heart attack occurs when the supply of blood to the heart is cut off.
+ Heart disease is an umbrella term for several different conditions.
+ You may have heard heart disease referred to as coronary heart disease, coronary artery disease or cardiovascular disease.
+ Angina is chest pain caused by the restriction of the blood supply to the heart.

The good news

After five years of not smoking, the risk of heart disease halves. After ten years the risk falls to the same as that of a non-smoker.

Even if you've already been diagnosed with heart disease, it's still worth giving up.

Here are five reasons why:

1 Blood clots are less likely when you stop smoking.
2 The heart is under less strain, so can pump blood and oxygen around the body with less effort.
3 Stopping smoking after a heart attack can reduce the risk of a second attack by half.
4 Stopping smoking can relieve angina.
5 If you have to have surgery for your smoking-related illness, you will recover better if you don't smoke.

HEALTH BENEFITS

Activity

Your body is a temple!

By sticking with the programme this far, your body is already beginning to repair itself. How many of the following benefits can you tick? See if you can add three more.

1 Improved breathing.

2 More stamina.

3 Smoker's cough has gone.

4 Sense of taste and smell have improved.

5 Breath, hair and skin don't smell of stale smoke.

6 Feel positive about lowering risk of disease.

7 Feel good about myself for stopping.

8 ....

9 ....

10 ....

Did you know?

People married to smokers, or exposed to tobacco smoke at work, have a 50–60 per cent increased risk of developing heart disease or suffering a stroke. Give up for your own sake – and for the sake of people around you. (There's more on passive smoking later in the programme.)

HEALTH BENEFITS

If you've embarked on a programme to get fit as you've followed the 100-day programme, you'll hopefully have noticed that you're less out of breath when you exercise than you were when you smoked.

TOP TIP

- If you've joined a gym, arrange a follow-up fitness check six weeks into your exercise programme. It will mean that you can measure your progress, see how far you've come and decide what you need to work on.

By giving up smoking now, you've hopefully spared yourself from irreparably damaging your lungs. There are lots of statistics available about smoking-related fatalities, but people often forget that smoking can have a permanently disabling effect, without actually killing you.

Ill health from smoking

Emphysema

Emphysema is a slowly progressing destruction of the lungs, which makes breathing very difficult. This is what happens to a smoker's lungs.

The bronchioles (small air-carrying tubes) become clogged with mucus. Air gets trapped in the alveoli (grape-like clusters at the end of the bronchioles). This can cause these tiny air sacs in the lungs to pop open. With broken air sacs, the lungs can't exchange oxygen for carbon dioxide efficiently. The elastic tissue that allows the lungs to stretch gets destroyed. Without stretchy fibres, the lungs find it difficult to expand and contract. At first, breathing may only be restricted at certain times of the day or during certain activities. But as less and less oxygen is transferred to the bloodstream, breathing becomes permanently difficult.

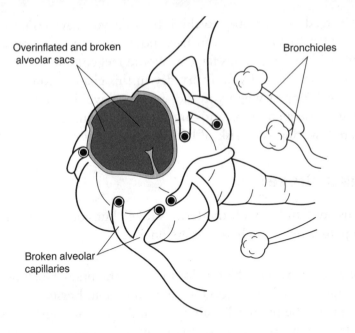

Overinflated and broken
alveolar sacs

Bronchioles

Broken alveolar
capillaries

Chronic bronchitis

Bronchitis means inflammation of the bronchi – the main airways that lead from the trachea (windpipe) into the lungs. Chronic bronchitis is an unpleasant and ongoing condition and a slow deterioration is likely. Heavy smokers may get emphysema and bronchitis together.

The two conditions are often referred to as chronic obstructive pulmonary disease, or COPD. There is no cure.

Activity
Labelling the lungs

- Study the picture of part of the lungs showing emphysema.

- Cover the picture over and see if you can accurately label the bronchioles, damaged alveolear capillaries and air sacs.

- Imagine you're a doctor. Could you explain what emphysema is to a smoker?

HEALTH BENEFITS

Before you read Day 67, stop to think how far you have come since your Quit Day. At QD +55, you have now been a non-smoker for two months. If you've got this far, you should feel confident that your smoking days are behind you. Every day in this chapter you can feel glad that you stopped when you did, and have avoided some of the devastating consequences of smoking. As well as lung and heart disease, you're lowering your risk of having a stroke by giving up.

What is a stroke?

Most of us are familiar with the term 'stroke', but could you explain what happens when somebody suffers one?

◆ A stroke occurs when a blood clot forms in the brain, blocking the blood supply, or when a blood vessel in the brain bursts.
◆ This deprives the brain cells of oxygen and other nutrients, causing them permanent damage or killing them off.
◆ The effects of a stroke can leave sufferers permanently disabled.
◆ A third of all stroke victims die within a year of the attack.
◆ Smoking increases your risk of stroke as the chemicals found in cigarettes can lead to a narrowing and furring of the arteries. This increases the chances of a blood clot becoming lodged in an artery in the brain.

Checklist

You're doing well, but don't forget that your body and mind are still adjusting to being a non-smoker. Be aware of danger zones. Cravings can still strike at any time and it's important not to forget how you coped with them in the past, when they were more frequent.

1 Prepare yourself before any social situation with a quick pep talk about how you're not going to smoke, even if you have a craving.
2 Refresh your distraction techniques – you never know when you'll need to call on them.
3 Feel proud, but don't be complacent.

Activity
Smoking and strokes

Test your knowledge.

1 Each year in the UK, what proportion of strokes are linked to smoking?

   a) 10 per cent

   b) 25 per cent

   c) 60 per cent

2 If you smoke less than ten cigarettes a day, how much higher is your risk of having a stroke compared to a non-smoker?

   a) 2.5

   b) 4

   c) the same risk as a non-smoker

3 If you smoke more than 20 cigarettes a day, how much higher is your risk of having a stroke compared to a non-smoker?

   a) 2.5

   b) 4

   c) 6

4 The risk of stroke for pipe and cigar smokers is less than the risk to cigarette smokers?

   True

   False

Answers:
1 – b) 2 – a) 3 – b) 4 – True. (But pipe and cigar smokers still face double the risk of having a stroke than a non-smoker.)

HEALTH BENEFITS

Are you concentrating?! Can you find the major disease risks associated with smoking? They're all contained in the word search. Words can go up, down or diagonally.

Key:
Heart disease
Emphysema
Bronchitis
Stroke
Lung cancer

C	A	I	M	L	C	G	D	I	B	O	M	E	A
S	I	T	I	H	C	N	O	R	B	E	S	K	E
C	F	Y	T	J	G	K	L	E	C	A	V	O	S
M	A	V	E	P	U	S	C	T	E	R	E	R	I
W	S	H	F	G	N	O	I	S	M	N	L	T	G
E	W	I	A	L	P	O	I	E	P	O	D	S	N
V	Y	T	I	S	A	D	E	B	H	Q	A	V	I
S	F	G	H	L	T	E	T	I	Y	U	E	R	B
G	A	W	M	R	C	S	P	O	S	T	Q	W	A
N	I	B	A	S	W	E	U	O	E	R	Y	F	O
V	U	E	W	D	T	N	H	E	M	N	S	W	L
P	H	F	E	L	U	N	G	C	A	N	C	E	R
E	N	I	R	G	K	L	F	P	I	A	S	R	T

These are not the only diseases that you are at risk from because of smoking.

In the rest of this chapter, the programme will take a look at some of the lesser-known effects that smoking has on different parts of the body.

Stomach

Smokers are more likely to get stomach ulcers, although researchers aren't really sure why. The ulcers are also made worse by smoking as experts believe the nicotine aggravates the lining of the stomach, making it more inflamed. Smoking will also speed up the rate at which your stomach digests food. This means you may experience diarrhoea the morning after smoking too much on a night out.

(**No more excuses!**)

(11) **I think smoking is glamorous, whatever anyone says.**

Maybe you saw someone famous smoking and thought they looked good? They won't look quite so good when the effects on their health kick in though, will they? Instead of carrying a picture that impresses you around in your head, think of the person you admire lying in a hospital bed, unable to breathe and riddled with smoking-related disease. That's not such a cool image is it? PS – Teenagers! You may think you look cool but nobody else does. Young people who smoke look rather stupid.

In the stars

Pictures of models and celebrities on TV and in magazines are often touched up or airbrushed to create an illusion of a perfect person. In reality even people who make a living from their good looks have bits about themselves they don't like. Few people are free of spots or wrinkles or flabby bits. You can try to change the things you don't like (you've proved that by giving up smoking), but have the wisdom to accept the things that can't be changed.

Activity

Think about your body

- Take a few minutes to think about your body. What are the physical aspects of your body that you like best?

    1 ....

    2 ....

    3 ....

- Now think of the organs on the inside of your body. Which do you consider the most important?

    1 ....

    2 ....

    3 ....

- When you eat and drink, think about what you're putting into your system. Write down everything you've eaten today and check that you're sticking to your new healthy diet regime and not slipping into bad habits.

HEALTH BENEFITS

Oral cancers

Oral cancers are cancers that affect any part of the lips, mouth, tongue and throat. They often go undiagnosed because the initial signs are painless and sufferers often avoid consulting a doctor, out of fear.

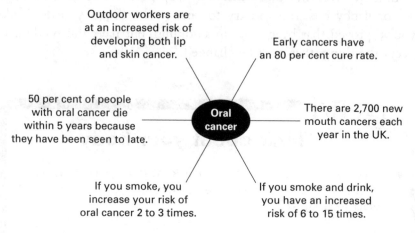

Outdoor workers are at an increased risk of developing both lip and skin cancer.

Early cancers have an 80 per cent cure rate.

50 per cent of people with oral cancer die within 5 years because they have been seen to late.

Oral cancer

There are 2,700 new mouth cancers each year in the UK.

If you smoke, you increase your risk of oral cancer 2 to 3 times.

If you smoke and drink, you have an increased risk of 6 to 15 times.

Source: www.wessexcancer.org

What to look for

As part of your new fit and healthy regime, you should be spending extra time taking care of your mouth and teeth. This will ensure that if there are any abnormalities in your mouth, you'll spot them quickly.

Five symptoms of oral cancer:

1 mouth ulcers that refuse to heal
2 a whitish or reddish patch anywhere in the mouth (this can be painless)
3 swelling under the neck or chin
4 difficulty chewing
5 a persistent feeling that something is caught in the throat.

Like all other cancers, early diagnosis and treatment is essential. Check with your GP if you were a heavy smoker and are worried you may have some of the symptoms.

Activity

Oral mouth examination

Stand in front of a mirror in a well-lit room to perform the oral examination. Follow these steps:

Neck (head back)
With your head tilted back, look for masses or lumps.

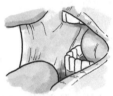

Cheeks
Use your thumb and forefinger to pull your cheeks away from your teeth.

Neck (head upright)
With your head upright, try to feel both sides of your neck and under your jaw.

Palate
Open wide to see the back and roof of your mouth.

Lips
Feel the inside and outside of your lip, using your thumb and forefinger. Also look carefully as you do this.

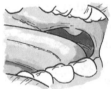

Tongue
Grab the end of your tongue with a tissue or gauze. Pull your tongue out, right and left, and examine each surface.

Gums
With your lips pulled away, examine all the gums.

Tongue (upward)
Raise the tip of your tongue to the roof of your mouth. Check the floor of your mouth and under your tongue.

HEALTH BENEFITS

The difference between men and women

Well, there are plenty of differences between men and women of course! But when it comes to smoking, women are at particular risk of damage to their health. Guys! This doesn't mean you can skip a few pages.

Here are five reasons why:

1 The more you read about how smoking damages the human body, male and female, the more likely you are to be put off starting up again.
2 Smoking when pregnant is a big health risk, but babies have fathers as well as mothers! If you're a man, support your partner.
3 Men may not get pregnant, but smoking around babies and children can have devastating consequences. Protect your family.
4 Smoking has a detrimental rate on fertility – for men and women.
5 Men and women may find that different methods of giving up smoking are more effective, depending on their sex.

Arm yourself with all the information that you can and you'll stand a better chance of staying stopped.

> **Did you know?**
>
> In Scotland, women are more likely to die of lung cancer than of any other type of cancer.

Activity

Women versus men

An American research project suggests that giving up smoking may be harder for women than for men. Get a friend of the opposite sex (preferably one who's given up or is giving up) to answer the following questions at the same time as you. Complete the quiz without conferring. When you've finished, discuss your answers. Speaking from experience, do you agree or disagree with the research?

1 Women smokers are more fearful of gaining weight when they quit than men.

   Agree/Disagree

2 Women's craving for cigarettes vary according to their menstrual cycle.

   Agree/Disagree

3 Husbands are less supportive of wives who try to give up than the other way around.

   Agree/Disagree

4 Women are more susceptible to environmental smoking factors – such as the need to smoke with particular friends or smoking with specific moods.

   Agree/Disagree

5 Women enjoy the feeling of control associated with having a cigarette.

   Agree/Disagree

HEALTH BENEFITS

Smoking and pregnancy

Many women lose the urge to smoke when they find out that they're pregnant. That's great if you're in that category, but it's not the same for everyone. Feeling guilty about smoking when you're pregnant won't help, so don't waste time on it. Instead, we're going to spend a couple of days looking at some of the facts about smoking at this time, to explain why it's so important to stop.

☉ TOP TIP

- If you're part of a couple who's expecting a baby, read this part of the programme together. Even if it's only one of you who's working through the programme, moral support is invaluable.

If you're not pregnant or considering a baby, it's still good to broaden your knowledge. So read on.

Men: More cigarettes smoked = more cases of impotence.

Did you know?

Smoking affects the fertility of both men and women.

Forget about thinking how sexy you look as a smoker – cigarettes are having the opposite effect on your virility. More women will be attracted to you as a non-smoker. Quit! For a long and happy sex life.

Women: More cigarettes = less chance of getting pregnant.

Female smokers:

◆ have a 30 per cent lower fertility rate than non-smokers
◆ are 3.4 times more likely to take more than a year to conceive
◆ go through the menopause two years earlier than non-smokers, on average.

What separates the quitters from the women who continue to smoke while they're pregnant? As a group, quitters aren't necessarily stronger or more intelligent – and it doesn't mean they love their babies more. They've simply set themselves up for success – which is what you're doing by following the 100-day programme.

'The sheer scale of damage that smoking causes to reproductive and child health is shocking. Men who think they might want children one day should bin cigarettes.' Dr Vivienne Nathanson, British Medical Association

Did you know?

If you give up smoking a year before trying for a family, your chances of conceiving return to the same as a non-smoking woman, according to the Imperial Cancer Research Fund.

Activity
Iron out the creases

It's likely that even so far into the programme, you still fancy a cigarette sometimes. It's important to keep working on techniques that distract you from wanting a cigarette. Think of a time of day when you still feel like a cigarette. To take your mind off it, do the ironing instead! If you never iron, it's about time you learned. Everyone should be capable of basic lifeskills and you have your new image to live up to.

HEALTH BENEFITS

These are the reasons why it's so important not to smoke if you're pregnant, or even if you're near to a woman who's pregnant:

Smoking – risk to mother

◆ Miscarriage
◆ Bleeding
◆ Nausea.

Smoking – risk to baby

◆ Reduced birth weight
◆ Premature birth
◆ Stillbirth.

Foetuses that don't grow well are more likely to be short of oxygen and need an emergency delivery. They can suffer breathing disorders, coughing, phlegm and wheezing and are more likely to develop asthma than if their parents don't smoke. Smoking is associated with decreased physical and poor intellectual development in children whose parents smoke.

Activity

For women who aren't pregnant

If you're not pregnant, or not considering having a baby, think of someone you know who has children.

Ask if you can chat to their kids about smoking. Ask what it's like for them being in a smoky environment.

Their honest opinions should strengthen your resolve.

According to medical experts, if you stop smoking during pregnancy you will benefit from:

● less morning sickness

● fewer complications

● a more contented baby after birth.

Activity

For pregnant women

Consider what *you* think would be the best reasons to stop.

1 Imagine being able to buy an extra present for the baby with the money you save.

2 Imagine not getting negative looks from passers-by if you're smoking while pregnant or pushing a buggy.

3 Imagine telling your doctor, health visitor or midwife that you've given up.

Can you think of two more good reasons? You may have reasons that are personal to you and your family.

4 ....

5 ....

Activity

For soon to be dads

Answer the following questions about planning for your baby's arrival.

Make your answers as detailed as you can.

1 What changes will you be making around the house? Perhaps you're decorating a nursery or buying a new cot?

2 When people congratulate you on becoming a future parent, how do you feel?

3 What three things are you looking forward to most about your new baby's arrival?

HEALTH BENEFITS

153

Smoking and cot death

It's unbearable to think about losing a child. But smoking both during pregnancy and around babies once they're born significantly increases the risk of cot death or SIDS (Sudden Infant Death Syndrome). SIDS occurs most often in infants between the ages of two and four months, while the baby is sleeping.

- The risk of cot death is trebled in cases where the mother of a baby smokes.
- If both mother and father smoke during the pregnancy, the baby is eight times more likely to die of cot death than if neither parent smokes.

'There is no doubt whatsoever that exposing babies to tobacco smoke and nicotine is highly dangerous. Do not smoke during pregnancy and never expose babies to tobacco smoke after they are born.' Spokeswoman, The Foundation for the Study of Infant Deaths

Smoking partners

If you're pregnant and your partner is reluctant to give up smoking, try talking to him about the information in this section of the programme. You could also mention the following points:

◆ Point out that it's his baby too. In fairness, he should try to give up.

◆ Explain that this is an exciting time in *both* of your lives, and it's important to share the whole experience (including giving up fags for the baby's sake).

◆ Make sure your partner understands that his smoking will have an effect on your baby's health, even if you've stopped.

Activity

Baby matters

Have a conversation with your partner, family or friends about what you think would be the best means of encouraging pregnant women not to smoke. Do you favour shock tactics such as harrowing advertising campaigns, or low-key educational methods? Don't make the discussion personal. Imagine you are a politician who has been given the task of improving women's health.

HEALTH BENEFITS

You're now entering the final quarter of the 100-day programme. Take a few moments to think about how you're feeling and how much you've already achieved by sticking with it. Re-energise your commitment to the programme today.

◆ Stay focused.
◆ Remember your reasons for giving up smoking.
◆ Research shows that the clearer people are about their motives, the more chance they have of success.

Activity

Reasons for giving up

Without referring to any lists you made earlier in the programme, write yourself a new list of five reasons you are giving up smoking. When you've finished, refer back to the original list you made in your notebook when you first started out on the programme.

1 ....
2 ....
3 ....
4 ....
5 ....

Have your reasons changed as you've progressed or are they still the same?

◆ Be positive and confident that you can quit.
◆ You have spent time and energy planning how you will deal with the task you're undergoing.
◆ You can and will do it if you persevere.
◆ Tens of thousands of people are quitting every day around the world.
◆ You can be one of them!

Quiz

If you've got this far and haven't had a cigarette, or a drag on some-one else's cigarette since your Quit Day, that's fantastic. So fantastic that you can skip this additional activity! If you've relapsed once or twice, but picked yourself up and got back on the programme, it shows you're still very much in control. Answer these questions to see how you've handled any ups and downs.

When you had a relapse cigarette did you:

a) think 'I've blown it,' I might as well smoke a few more
b) react calmly and try to understand why you'd smoked
c) spend the next week beating yourself up and feeling like a failure?

The first puff on a cigarette after giving up for a time made you feel:

a) wonderful
b) light-headed
c) disgusted.

The next time you had a craving after relapsing you:

a) remembered you regretted your last relapse and avoided it
b) distracted yourself and avoided it
c) thought 'what the hell!' and smoked it anyway.

Your score

If you scored mostly a) or c) – Frequent relapses make giving up hard-er because they damage your self-esteem. Be sure you really want to give up and strengthen your resolve.

If you answered mostly b) – You've handled your relapses confidently, well done!

TOP TIP

- Browse through your no-smoking notebook every so often. It's where you've recorded all your thoughts and feelings about making a significant change to your life. If you ever doubt yourself, all the motivation you need is there.

HEALTH BENEFITS

Your notes

CHAPTER 6

PASSIVE SMOKING

Throughout Chapter 5 we concentrated on learning about the unpleasant consequences of smoking on your own body, which you're now free of. Even if you used to dismiss smoking-related diseases as something that would never happen to you when you were a smoker, it must feel good to feel fit and healthy now. In this chapter we're going to look at the effect smoking has on the people around you.

Activity

Phone a friend!

It's not good to obsess about giving up smoking and to talk about it endlessly with friends, family and colleagues. But it is important to make sure you have every possible trick up your sleeve to make sure you don't relapse.

- Find someone who has successfully given up smoking – it won't be too hard if you ask around – for suggestions as to how they've done it.

- Explain that you are more than halfway through the 100-day programme and doing well.

- Pick the other person's brains – ask if they have any tips that they found helpful when they were giving up.

- Ask how they feel about being in a smoky environment, now that they don't smoke.

TOP TIP

- Choose a friend who you don't talk to every day. You're looking for fresh ideas.

Most ex-smokers find the effects of passive smoking unpleasant. By this stage in the programme, you should no longer need to deliberately avoid smoky venues, as long as you take care of your alcohol intake. How do you feel about other people's smoke? Ideally, you'll find it unpleasant. If you still crave being in a smoky atmosphere, be extra vigilant about relapsing. It suggests you're still eager to inhale.

Did you know?

● The non-smoking partner of a smoker develops a quarter of the harmful effects the smoker will experience.

● The partner of a 20-a-day smoker smokes the equivalent of five cigarettes a day.

● Five cigarettes a day increases disease rates by between 12 and 25 per cent.

Passive smoking

◆ 10,000 non-smokers a year die in the UK from passive smoking.

◆ Many of them work in the hospitality industry.

◆ Some of the immediate effects of passive smoking include eye irritation, headache, cough, sore throat, dizziness and nausea.

◆ Adults with asthma can experience a significant decline in lung function when exposed to second-hand cigarette smoke.

◆ 30 minutes of exposure is enough to reduce coronary blood flow in a non-smoking adult.

Why is passive smoking dangerous?

There are two types of smoke that the passive smoker inhales:

◆ *Sidestream* smoke is smoke from the burning tip of a cigarette.
◆ *Mainstream* smoke is smoke that has been inhaled, then exhaled by the nearby smoker.
◆ Tobacco smoke contains over 4,000 chemicals in the form of particles and gases.
◆ Many potentially toxic gases are present in higher concentrations in sidestream smoke than in mainstream smoke.
◆ Nearly 85 per cent of the smoke in a room results from sidestream smoke.
◆ In America, sidestream smoke has been classified as a Class A carcinogen by the Environmental Protection Agency.
◆ Other Class A carcinogens include asbestos, arsenic, benzene and radon gas.

Smoking around children

Passive smoking is bad for adults, but it can have a devastating effect on children. Unlike adults, children don't have a choice about whether or not they're exposed to tobacco smoke. Children whose parents smoke are far more likely to develop asthma than the children of non-smoking parents. Smoking in a separate room of the house doesn't mean children are less at risk.

Survey by the Doctor Patient Partnership

● 42 per cent of children live in a home where at least one person smokes.
● 23 per cent of parents questioned had no idea that smoking has an adverse affect on their children's health.
● 72 per cent of the respondents (including some smokers) said smoking should be banned in households with children.

PASSIVE SMOKING

- 17,000 children under the age of five are admitted to hospital every year because of the effects of passive smoking.
- Children who live in a household where both parents smoke receive a nicotine equivalent of 80 cigarettes per day.

'The only way for parents to protect their children from tobacco smoke is by making their homes entirely smoke free.' Deborah Arnott, anti-smoking campaigner

Smoking and pets

Your pets suffer from passive smoking too, but owners often have no idea that smoking near their animals causes them distress. Animals suffer irritation to the eyes and their breathing can be affected in the same way as passive smoking affects humans. Try not to smoke when your pet is sitting nearby.

Activity
The effect on your loved ones

- Think of someone you love who doesn't smoke. This can be an adult, a child or a pet.

- Imagine them inhaling your cigarette smoke when they don't want to.

- How do you feel about the fact that you are responsible for causing them harm?

TOP TIP

- Still coughing, even though you've given up? Try a herbal remedy. Neal's Yard Clear Lung Tea is made with sage and elderflower and has helped lots of people to soothe a tickly cough. Phone 0845 2623145 to order.

PASSIVE SMOKING

Even if you don't live with children, there are plenty of good reasons to make your house a smoke-free zone. According to estate agents, your house price will plummet if you're a smoker. The smell of stale smoke gets everywhere – and it's the first thing prospective buyers will notice when they step through your front door. First impressions are very important. Smokers won't notice it because they're accustomed to the smell, but if you're trying to sell, then a fresh-smelling, unstained home will be far more appealing to potential buyers.

But I don't intend to sell my house!

If this is how you react to reading the above paragraph, check that your commitment to the programme isn't wavering. Remember, smokers always have an excuse ready for why they still smoke. Make sure you're not slipping into old habits of negative thought processes. It doesn't matter if your house isn't on the market. As a non-smoker, you want to live in the nicest environment possible – because you're worth it!

Activity

Smell the smoke

Your own sense of smell (and taste) will have improved since you stopped smoking. But it may be that you don't notice the smell of stale smoke in your house, because you've been living with it for so long. Invite a non-smoking friend round for a drink one evening and, while they're there, ask them for an honest opinion on how smoky your home smells to them.

No more excuses!

(12) I smoke because it's a reward after a long day.

Rewards are little treats that brighten up your life. Cigarettes don't brighten your life – they detract from it – and often pull people into a cycle of self loathing. You need to think up some other rewards (and this doesn't mean chocolates!)

Bringing your home up to date needn't cost a fortune – everyone is into DIY these days and there's plenty of help at hand if you're a first-timer. If you need some help with painting or decorating, why not make it into a social occasion. Friends, family and neighbours will be happy to help if you give them some notice and promise them a glass of wine, a home-cooked meal, or a favour in return.

CHECK ✔

This week I have:

◆ written a list of the things I *disliked* about smoking that moti-vated me to give up
◆ looked forward to reaching the end of the programme by trying the visualisation technique on Day 62.

PASSIVE SMOKING

In this chapter we've learned about the benefits that you giving up smoking has for the people close to you. It should feel good that your determination to stick with the 100-day programme has such far-reaching consequences. When you get to Day 100 (and it's not long now!), you'll be a confident non-smoker. As the months and years go by, it will feel more and more natural that you don't smoke.

Creating a non-smoking home will ensure that there are no reminders of your past life as a smoker. You don't need to rush into a big DIY job today – it will require planning and you'll need to set aside time when you're able to commit to doing the jobs that need doing effectively. It doesn't matter if you share a property and have just one room of your own to concentrate on, or if you live in a big house. You can start today by taking a good look at walls, objects and floorings and working out where you can freshen up and make changes. It doesn't mean spending lots of money. You can work on your environment over time.

 TOP TIP

- Temporarily removing paintings will show up how nicotine stains have discoloured the walls.

Overwhelmed?

Don't feel daunted if it seems that a lot of work needs doing. Make a list of specific tasks of manageable sizes. For example, 'Take sitting room curtains to dry cleaners' will seem more achievable than a vague note that says 'Decorate downstairs'.

'Avoiding the phrase "I don't have time..." will soon help you to realise that you do have the time needed for just about anything you choose to accomplish in life.' Bo Bennett, writer

PASSIVE SMOKING

Five reasons for a DIY home makeover

1 Giving up smoking is a life-changing event.
2 Changing your surroundings will confirm that you've moved on.
3 Learning DIY will give you new skills and keep your mind off cigarettes.
4 You'll feel proud when you see the results you can achieve.
5 You'll no longer associate your home with somewhere you smoked.

Activity

Home audit

Take your no-smoking notebook and a pen and go around each room in your home. If you share a home, it's a task you can do together. Tackle your audit in the same way that you updated your wardrobe. Giving up cigarettes is all about throwing out the old and bringing in the new.

Make a list for each room. Pay particular attention to walls, floors and objects that have been affected by smoke. Plan to:

- clean removable fabrics like curtains, sofa covers and cushions

- replace stained or stale-smelling lampshades

- shampoo carpets

- paint walls

- give permanent fixtures such as kitchen and bathroom cupboards and fittings a really good spring clean.

PASSIVE SMOKING

Giving your house a makeover will take time but can be very satisfying. And after you've successfully completed the 100-day programme, a beautiful smoke–free home will last you well into the future. Keep today's guide to DIY handy for when you begin (DIY tips from www.upmystreet.com).

Plan properly

◆ Before you begin, be clear about what you want to achieve.
◆ Buy some home decorating magazines for inspiration and tips.
◆ Be realistic about the time a job will take. You'll need to factor in clearing a room, washing down paintwork and covering surfaces before you even begin decorating.
◆ Always get sample paint pots and swatches to see how your proposed colours work in the room both in daylight and artificial light.
◆ Plan sensibly. Paint before cleaning the carpet or getting new furniture delivered.

Don't get carried away!

It's possible to create a fresh new look for your smoke-free home without making big changes. But if you do decide to put your energy as a fully fledged non-smoker into some serious work on your property – make sure you seek professional advice for any structural alterations you're considering. Some types of work need planning permission from the council. Do your research.

Do a proper budget

Be realistic about your budget and where you can economise. While you may be able to paint the room, more specialised jobs are best left to the professionals.

Shop around

Don't rely just on the big-name DIY stores for your paint and tools. Local trade shops often offer a better deal.

PASSIVE SMOKING

TOP TIP

- Think carefully about colours if you're painting walls. Perhaps quitting the fags has lifted your spirits so much that you feel like choosing bright colours that express your new mood.

Activity

How have you changed?

Write down three ways you think your attitude to life has changed since you gave up smoking. Anyone who has given up deserves to feel a wonderful sense of achievement, but what else have you noticed? Perhaps you feel more confident, or realise that you don't need to smoke a cigarette to fit into a new group?

1 ....

2 ....

3 ....

Now ask a friend or partner to tell you some of the differences they've noticed in you since you gave up.

Did you know?

80 per cent of smokers want to quit the habit. The reason so many people are doing something they don't want to do is because of the physical addiction that subsequently causes psychological dependence. You've broken the physical addiction and are learning to break the psychological addiction every day that goes by. For most readers it will have been a long struggle. Never, ever go back to being a smoker.

PASSIVE SMOKING

Giving up smoking is all about changing attitudes about how you see yourself and how you see the world around you. A good way to check if you've really put smoking behind you is to take a look at how you react to other smokers, and to campaigns that encourage people to quit.

Activity

Then and now

- Think back to when you used to smoke.

- In your notebook, draw a line down the centre of the page to make two columns. Mark the first **Then** and the second **Now**.

- Answer the following questions, which are about how you react to the smoking messages that we see in everyday life. For example:

  1 How did/do you react to health warnings on cigarette packets?

Then	**Now**
Didn't notice them.	They seem huge!

Here are the rest of the questions. How did/do you react to:

  2 A pregnant woman smoking?

  3 A no-smoking sign in a café?

  4 A designated smokers' area in an airport terminal?

  5 Anti-smoking television and poster adverts?

  6 A friend telling you they've given up smoking?

7 Ticking a smoker/non-smoker box on an official form?

8 Asking for a smoking/non-smoking table in a restaurant?

9 Somebody smoking very close to you?

10 The ban on smoking in public places?

How do your answers differ? The second column should be a lot more positive. Take a careful look at your answers and see if there are any that cast doubt on your non-smoking status. For example, if in the 'Now' column of Question 10 you've written 'I'm not sure about it', you need to retrace your steps and build on the positive reasons for giving up and the aspects of quitting that you benefit from and enjoy.

Saying no

◆ Declining a cigarette only takes a split second, just as accepting one does.
◆ But if you decline, you'll feel good later, not cross with yourself.
◆ Smokers won't be surprised at you refusing their offer of a fag – they'll expect it – so don't let seeming unsociable be your worry.

If you don't give up smoking now, you risk spending the next months and years feeling under increasing pressure to give up – from everyone. It's a good enough reason in itself to ditch the fags. Who wants to feel like a social misfit and spend their lives apologising for a stupid habit?

Socialising, going to the pub, seeing friends and family, going on holiday or to a movie are all activities that are meant to be enjoyed. If you spend half the time wondering if you can smoke, or where you can smoke, or wanting to smoke, you'll be wasting the best of your free time.

TOP TIP

So even if you've had the odd relapse, remember:
- Don't panic.
- Keep trying and you will get there.
- Never give up trying to give up.
- Emergency tips for relapsing are on Day 26!

The impact of health warnings

Governments spend money on health warnings and no-smoking campaigns because … they work.

- The larger the health warning message, the more effective it is in getting people to quit.
- Large-print health warnings have most impact on persuading people not to take up smoking and least impact on hardcore smokers.
- Smokers over the age of 30 are more scared by health warnings than younger people.
- The three most effective warnings on cigarette packets are:
SMOKING KILLS
SMOKING CAUSES CANCER
SMOKING WHEN PREGNANT HARMS YOUR BABY

Some television campaigns about smoking are very harrowing. They show smokers who are facing death talking about how they regret having smoked, and children of smokers crying because a parent has a smoking-related illness. You may think these adverts are too explicit, but they do use real people – not actors – to get the point across. Next time you see one, look beyond the pictures. If you tend to dismiss them, make yourself think about the message they're trying to convey. To give up smoking, you have to wake up to the fact that it's killing you.

Activity

Stop-smoking messages

During the day today, count every single message you see that relates to giving up smoking. Whether you're driving, walking to work or at the shops, you're bound to see several images that tell you 'Smoking Kills'.

Total: ....

Why would you ignore them?

....

....

PASSIVE SMOKING

In 2004, the Irish Republic introduced a total ban on smoking in workplaces and public spaces. The ban was declared a success after its first year in place. Next in line is Northern Ireland, where smoking will be banned in all workplaces and enclosed public spaces by 2007. This includes pubs, bars and restaurants. A smoking ban in the rest of UK will come into effect once the legislation has been finalised in Parliament.

'Smoking is your choice. You have every right to live your life as you choose. But nobody has the right to subject colleagues and non-smoking members of the public to the dangers of second-hand smoke.' Shaun Woodward, Health Minister (and ex-smoker)

Smoking bans in public places are becoming more commonplace and, because of the cost to people's lives and to health services, governments will continue to campaign against smoking. Save yourself the stigma! Stick with giving up, even if you're still surprised by a craving sometimes.

No more excuses!

 I smoke because it helps me to fit in.

If you're holding on to this as a reason, it's time to wake up! The person who doesn't fit in at a social occasion these days is the person who smokes. Most public entertainment venues have banned smoking, and more and more homeowners insist their smoking guests go outside to have a cigarette. If you're the only smoker in a group, the others may be looking at you with pity. After all, you're being controlled by something, while they're independent and in control.

Where is smoking banned?

California – 1998
New York – 2003
India – 2004

Activity

Have your say

What's your opinion on smoking bans? Make a list of advantages and disadvantages of a total smoking ban in public venues and discuss them with a friend. Follow these tips:

- Remember that in this section of the programme, we're checking how confident you are that you're a genuine non-smoker.

- Be honest, but be aware what a committed ex-smoker or somebody who has never smoked would have to say on the subject.

- How would their opinions differ to yours?

- If you are very opposed to the idea, think why.

- Is it because you feel strongly about the imposition of certain laws, or is it because you still fear going to the pub and not being able to have a fag with your drink?

Did you know?

91 per cent of those questioned in Northern Ireland were in favour of a total ban on smoking in public places, according to a government consultation paper. But FOREST, a group that campaigns for people to be allowed to smoke, put the figure at just 33 per cent.

PASSIVE SMOKING

Smokers often react against campaigns to encourage them to give up by blaming the 'nanny state'. There may be lots of reasons that you feel the government tries to control the way you live in a way you don't like, but when it comes to smoking, Britain is not alone in clamping down.

Activity

Around the world quiz

Look at the descriptions of the following countries and their policies on smoking. Can you match the name to the country from the list below?

Bhutan France Canada Iran Australia Netherlands

1 In this country, smoking is banned in all airports, government offices and workplaces. Most restaurants and shopping centres are also smoke-free zones. There is a total ban on smoking in one popular tourist area.

2 This country has some of the lowest smoking rates in the world. Smoking is banned in many workplaces and public places. Cigarette packets bear graphic images of the damage done to internal organs by smoking.

3 The government of this country tried to cut smoking levels by raising the price of cigarettes by 20 per cent in 2003. Tobacconists went on strike. The price hike made little difference to the numbers of people who smoke.

4 Smoking was banned in public buildings, including hotels and restaurants, in this country in 2003. Tobacco advertising was also banned. But laws are rarely enforced and statistics show that more and more young people are starting to smoke.

PASSIVE SMOKING

5 This country has one of the highest rates of smoking in the European Union. Its government introduced a tough crackdown on smoking in 2005. Bars and restaurants must enforce their own no-smoking policy or face a government-imposed ban.

6 This is the first country in the world to introduce a total ban on tobacco sales. All shops, hotels, restaurants and bars are no longer allowed to sell tobacco. There are severe penalties for those who flout the law.

7 Tobacco advertising and smoking in public places has been banned in this country. The sale of cigarettes to children has also been banned. But the laws are often flouted and there is poor enforcement.

Answers

1 Australia   2 Canada   3 France   4 Iran
5 Netherlands   6 Bhutan   7 India

TOP TIP

- If you need some extra motivation, think about where you might go for your next holiday. Imagine waiting for your plane at the airport and not worrying about when you should try to cram in your last cigarette before you board the plane and can't smoke. Giving up smoking sets you free. The world is your oyster!

PASSIVE SMOKING

Like smokers, tobacco manufacturers are fighting a losing battle for their cause. The evidence that smoking kills is so overwhelming that it's becoming increasingly hard for them to justify their product as something that will enhance people's lives.

Activity

I don't believe it!

- It's astonishing to look back and see how naïve everyone was about smoking at first. But towards the beginning of last century, there simply wasn't the medical research to inform us of the devastating effect smoking has on our health.
- For today's task, look at the following slogans. There are 3 Xs where the brand name of a cigarette would go. Were they really used in nationwide advertising campaigns or are they made up?

Answer True or False.

1 Many prominent athletes smoke XXX all day long with no harmful effects to wind or physical condition.   T/F
2 XXX – a cigarette recognised by eminent medical authorities for its advantages to the nose and throat.   T/F
3 More doctors smoke XXX than any other cigarette.   T/F
4 XXX renews and restores bodily energy.   T/F
5 No other cigarette approaches such a degree of health protection as XXX.   T/F

Answers

They're all true!
1 Lucky Strike, 1929.
2 Philip Morris, 1939.
3 Camel, 1946.
4 Camel, 1950.
5 Kent, 1952.

PASSIVE SMOKING

How times have changed

1940s – tobacco adverts claim that cigarettes enhance health and reduce risk of illness.

1950s – the Marlboro Man (one of the most successful adverts of all time) is born.

1960s – advertisers begin to deny that cigarettes cause cancer.

1970s – Marlboro Man is dropped from all UK advertising.

1980s – manufacturers start to claim advertising tobacco doesn't encourage people to take up smoking, only to change brand if they smoke already.

1990s – stricter advertising codes force manufacturers to use less overt, abstract images to promote their cigarettes.

2003 – tobacco advertising is banned in the UK.

The Western world has six major tobacco companies. They are: Rothmans, BAT Industries, Imperial Tobacco, Phillip Morris, RJ Reynolds and American Brands. The first three are based in the UK. Think back to when you smoked. Did you know who was manufacturing your cigarettes?

Did you know?

In the UK, linking tobacco adverts with sexual prowess, heroism and alcohol was disallowed in the 1970s.

TOP TIP

- Remember to practise a deep breathing exercise or a visualisation technique regularly.

PASSIVE SMOKING

The main reason for giving up smoking is simply that we know how bad it is for us. Within that bracket, individual people will have personal reasons to stop. But let's take a look at the broader picture for a moment. Step outside your own world and see the effect that cigarettes have on people in other countries – especially developing countries. Not everybody in the world has access to the information about health risks that we take for granted in the West. You may not like constantly hearing how bad smoking is for you, but isn't it better to know the risks and make an informed choice about whether you continue to smoke or not?

♦ Smoking is steadily increasing in developing countries.
♦ There are no health warnings on the cigarettes sold in developing countries.
♦ Some cigarettes sold to countries in Asia, Africa and Latin America deliver twice as much tar as the same brands that are sold in the countries where they're manufactured.
♦ There are no advertising and sponsorship controls in developing countries.
♦ Smoking is portrayed as a sophisticated Western habit, which encourages people to take it up.
♦ Between 1985 and 1987 US tobacco exports to Asia increased by more than 91 per cent.
♦ A dramatic rise in smoking in some poorer countries has been linked to a big increase in tobacco advertising designed to target young people and women.
♦ Hard-sell marketing techniques in developing countries have included handing out free cigarettes to children, and sponsoring nightclubs and discos.

The consequences

Smoking in poor countries can have a more far-reaching detrimental effect than in more affluent countries like Britain. The money you are saving by not smoking will enable you to buy some luxuries. But in countries where food is scarce, the more money people spend on cigarettes, the less they have for basic necessities like food and clothing. As the populations starts to suffer the ill-health consequences of smoking, the already over-stretched health services become less able to cope.

The farmers' dilemma

Tobacco companies offer farmers in developing countries seed, fertiliser, training and development loans (which trap the farmer into a cycle of debt). They guarantee the price plus prompt payment, thus making tobacco an attractive 'cash crop', which is often grown in place of much-needed food. This contributes to food shortages.

Activity

Donate to charity

- Make a donation to a charity that supports people less fortunate than yourself. This could be a one-off payment or a regular contribution.

- How about joining a scheme in which you give a small amount of money (it can be as little as a pound a month) to a charity on a regular basis? Look through newspapers, magazines, in the library or on the internet to find a charity that you would like to contribute to.

- Even donating a small proportion of the money you have saved on cigarettes will make a big difference to someone. Do some good and feel good about yourself at the same time.

PASSIVE SMOKING

Your notes

CHAPTER 7

PREPARING FOR THE FUTURE

Day 100 of the programme is now within sight!

Answer this question quickly?

When I get to QD +88 on Day 100 I will:

a) throw this book in the air and think, 'Hurray, it's all over!'
b) be quietly determined to continue putting into practice everything I have learned.

If you answered a) – go back to NS+1 immediately!

The reason the programme is spread out over 100 days is to ensure that the skills you have been building are sustainable. Over time, everything you have learned will become second nature. But before you turn the final page, we need to make sure that you've properly taken on board the key life changes that will help you to maintain a happy existence as a non-smoker.

During the programme there have been plenty of tips and motivation boosters to keep you from relapsing. All the way along, while your body has been adjusting to nicotine withdrawal, the priority has been to keep you from having a fag – by whatever means possible.

Activity Build a house!

Imagine you are going to build a house on a piece of land where the weather can be very hostile. It rains a lot and there are strong winds. You want the house to be sturdy enough to withstand the elements and last for a very long time.

Question: What is the single most important thing to ensure you build a strong house?

Answer: ....

Check you have written the right answer (at the bottom of the page) before reading on.

Like a house, you need strong foundations if the new you is to last a lifetime. Not smoking will continue to get easier, but the odd craving could strike like a freak gust of wind at any time!

There are the five crucial factors that will underpin your success. To remain a non-smoker, you need:

1 good self-esteem and an image of yourself you are proud of

2 a diet that makes you feel healthy, so you don't want to spoil that wellbeing

3 an ongoing exercise programme

4 new hobbies and interests to give you a purpose in life

5 learned-by-heart techniques that back up your determination (lifeskills).

In the last chapter of *Choker to Non-Smoker*, we're going to make absolutely sure that the tools that will keep you not smoking are firmly in place.

Activity answer: FOUNDATIONS

'Having a positive mental attitude is asking how something can be done rather than saying it can't be done.' Bo Bennett, writer

PREPARING FOR THE FUTURE

Self-esteem

All the time you were smoking, you were doing something that harmed you. Even if you didn't know it, this would have had a negative effect on your self-esteem. Giving up smoking should have given you a huge boost. Even if day-to-day life gets in the way, you should still be able to find a few moments every day to take a deep breath and think, 'I did it! Good for me!'

Activity

Check your self-esteem

Let's check that *is* the case.

Look at the following list. There are 15 statements. Tick any that apply to you.

- I try to avoid social situations – not just so that I don't have a cigarette, but because I feel awkward around other people.
- I have high levels of anxiety and emotional turmoil.
- My social skills aren't very good.
- I wonder if I may have an eating disorder.
- If I'm given a compliment, I put myself down, rather than accepting it graciously.
- I'm hard on myself.
- I dwell on the negative aspect of any situation.
- I feel very concerned about what people think of me.
- I don't look after myself well – I'll skip a bath or not wash my hair when I can get away with it.
- Although I don't treat myself well, I'm always good to other people.
- I worry if I've said the wrong thing to people and should apologise.
- I'm reluctant to take on new challenges.
- I'm very bad at making simple decisions.
- I don't expect much from life and don't expect to be successful in the things I do.
- I don't feel great that I've given up smoking.

Ideally, there won't be too many ticks when you've read through the list. But if more than five or six ring true, your self-esteem could probably do with some work. Some people seem to be effortlessly confident, but they're not really any different to anyone else. They've just learned the skills that enable them to live life effectively. You can do that too. You've made the biggest start by giving up smoking! If you feel permanently depressed, ask your GP for advice. Tell them that you've given up smoking and explain how unhappy you feel.

Confidence booster

Confidence comes from within. However many times somebody else tells you that you're wonderful, you won't feel good until you believe it yourself. Focus on your best points. Practice turning any negative thoughts that you have into positive thoughts – *every day*. This is a good model for improving confidence that everyone can benefit from, whether or not they have given up smoking.

TOP TIP

- Pin a photograph of yourself that you like on the fridge or the back of the bedroom door. Perhaps you like it because you're smiling, or because your hair looked great that day. If you doubt yourself, look at it!

CHECK ✔

This week I have:

◆ memorised how to say *no*, when somebody offers me a cigarette. (Check out Day 80!)

PREPARING FOR THE FUTURE

Self-esteem and confidence go hand in hand. Roughly speaking, you can think of self-esteem as how you feel about yourself and confidence as how you convey yourself to other people.

Confidence ABC

A Research shows that the more confident somebody is in themselves, the less they tend to use personal pronouns. These are words like 'me, myself, I, mine'.

♦ Try to focus your attention away from yourself, although not at the expense of your own needs. It's a question of getting the balance right.

B A person's mental and, even to some extent, physical health, can be directly related to how 'self-referential' they are in their conversation.

♦ Turning your attention towards other people will give you an interest in something outside yourself and, in turn, may make you more interesting to other people too!

C People who have low self-esteem react to success in a different way to naturally confident people. They tend to write off an achievement as good luck, chance or someone else's responsibility.

♦ Think of yourself as the confident, capable person that you are. Thinking positive is hard work sometimes, but it does work.

Activity
Body and mind

Spend half an hour on this activity. The idea is that you really see yourself in a positive light – and appreciate your achievement in giving up smoking. It's important to set time aside to do this. Busy lives can mean too little time in which to relax and think about ourselves.

● Lie on your back. Light some candles. Choose a time when it's quiet around you. It's a good exercise for the bath!

- Think of your body from top to toe.

- All thoughts must be positive.

- Start at the top by running your fingers through your clean hair.

- Your eyes are bright and smoke free.

- Your teeth are sparkly.

- Your breath is fresh.

- Your skin is healthy.

- Work down your body until you get to your toes.

Concentrate on what's happening on the inside as well.

- Oxygen is running freely through your clear, clean arteries.

- Your heart is pumping strongly.

- Breathe deeply. Pull the air into your clean, expansive lungs.

Your commitment

Make a commitment to regularly repeat the confidence-boosting activities you've learned throughout the 100-day programme.

Start a fresh page in your no-smoking notebook and write these words:

- I, ..., am a confident person.

- Think of improving your confidence and self-esteem as pouring the first layer of cement into the foundations of that house you're building.

- *Self-esteem – goal achieved.*

Diet

If you have put on a few pounds since you gave up smoking, it doesn't matter. Be realistic. Giving up is hard enough, and nobody can expect to cope with stop-smoking plans and diet plans all at the same time. But if your weight has been creeping up, it makes sense to put a system in place now, to keep it under control. Don't worry! Keeping what you eat in check is a matter of practice – people don't have a physical addiction to food in the way that they do to nicotine.

Activity

Test your nutrition IQ

The 100-day programme has shown you how to shift your diet to create a sustainable healthy eating plan. But how much do you know about what you eat and the effect it has on your body?

Answer True or False to the following five questions:

- Before exercising, you should stay away from sugary snacks and drinks because they'll give you an energy low during exercise.

  True/False

- After exercise, it would be better to eat a tuna sandwich than plain bread.

  True/False

- The 'recommended daily allowance' on food labels shows the minimum nutrient levels you should try to meet.

  True/False

- Frozen vegetables are less nutritious than fresh vegetables.

  True/False

- Whether you are a man or a woman, your waist measurement should equal your hip measurement.

  True/False

Answers

Question 1: False
Research shows that a chocolate bar or sugary sports drink consumed 30 minutes before exercise doesn't hamper performance and may even improve it. The crucial point is that you exercise immediately after the sugary snack.

Question 2: True
After exercising, it's best to combine protein (e.g. tuna) and carbohydrates (e.g. bread). This speeds up and replenishes essential glycogen in the body.

Question 3: True
They are minimum recommendations – you should try to take in a little more of these nutrients every day.

Question 4: False
These days, veg is frozen immediately after harvest and retains its goodness. In some cases, frozen veg may even contain more nutrients than 'fresh' produce that has been stored for a few days. By keeping a few packs of veg in the freezer, there's no excuse not to eat your 'five a day'.

Question 5: False
Your hips should be larger than your waist. If they aren't, you're probably carrying too much fat around your tummy. Fat seems to shift to the abdomen with age (you've heard of the 'middle aged spread'!). So there's another reason to keep eating well and exercising.

PREPARING FOR THE FUTURE

Diet continued

Make sure you're maximis-
ing the benefits of stopping
smoking by sustaining a
healthy lifestyle. In the same
way as not smoking will become second
nature, eating well needs to become a
part of your daily routine too.

Five main food groups

There are five main food groups. For a healthy diet you need to eat a
mixture of foods from each group.

1 Bread, potatoes, pasta, rice, noodles and breakfast cereals

These foods mostly contain starch and should be the main part of all
your meals.

2 Fruit and vegetables

These are all excellent sources of vitamins, minerals and fibre and are
naturally low in fat and calories.

3 Milk and dairy foods

Dairy products are rich in protein, calcium, vitamins and minerals.
Aim for two or three servings a day, maximum, because dairy can also
have a high fat content.

4 Meat, fish, poultry and pulses

It's good to eat oily fish (sardines, mackerel, salmon) a couple of times
a week. Red meat is an excellent source of iron and vitamin B12, but
choose leaner cuts and trim off all visible fat before cooking. Lentils,
nuts, peas and beans are also in this food group.

5 *Foods containing fats and sugars*

Think of this category as an occasional treat.

Activity

Dinner guest

- Imagine you're cooking for a famous person you admire. They're not a fussy eater, but they need to look good and will expect a healthy meal.

- Plan three healthy courses for them and write the menu in your no-smoking notebook. Make sure it contains a mix of all the food groups.

Alcohol

It's impossible to over-emphasise how difficult it is to break the link between alcohol and smoking. If you're going out for a drink, make sure you're well armed with all the techniques you have learned to distract yourself from having a cigarette. Crucially, remember that the more you drink, the more you're likely to think that you don't care if you smoke. BUT YOU DO!

TOP TIP

Aim to eat five portions of fruit and veg every day. Use an empty, standard-size mug as a rough measure.

- **Raw, leafy vegetables** 1 serving = one mug.
- **Dense vegetables** 1 serving = half a mug.
- **Fruit 1 serving** = the size of a medium apple.

PREPARING FOR THE FUTURE

Exercise

It's easy to start off on an exercise programme enthusiastically, but harder to maintain momentum over time. In the first few weeks you're more likely to feel the health benefits quickly, but as time goes by you may become despondent as you get used to feeling better.

But it's the long-term exercise that will really make a difference to your level of fitness, health and general sense of well being.

Check back to earlier in the programme when you first started exercising. How have you done since then?

Quick quiz

Which is more true to you? Cross out the answers that don't apply, leaving you with a list of true statements. Ignore the symbols at the end of each statement for now.

- I never really got into a pattern of regular exercise. (X)

- I discovered how much I enjoyed exercising. (*)

- I started off running/going to the gym, but lapsed after a few weeks. (X)

- I'm still exercising regularly. (*)

- I exercise for half an hour at least three times a week. (*)

- Sometimes I go for several days without exercise. (X)

- If I don't exercise for a few days, I miss it. (*)

- I don't feel noticeably better since I stopped smoking. (X)

- I've put on weight. (X)

- I don't have time to exercise. (X)

Are you left with more *s or more Xs?

When you look at the completed list, you'll probably be able to gauge for yourself how well you're doing. You need *s, not Xs. Don't give up. Exercise really can work for you – it's just a case of finding something that suits you.

TOP TIP

Remember – you're building foundations to keep you fit, healthy and happy in the future. You've made a commitment to work on your self-esteem and to eat healthily.
Regular exercise will support both of those things.

- If you don't exercise, you are more likely to feel guilty or bad about yourself.
- If you do exercise, you are more likely to feel like eating well.

Did you know?

Exercise releases endorphins into the body, which make you feel good. Even if you don't feel like it – do it anyway – it's guaranteed you'll feel pleased you made the effort.

Activity
Keep exercising!

Get out of the rut. If you haven't done any exercise today, do half an hour right now. Here are some suggestions to suit the time of day:

1 Go out for a brisk, half-hour walk.

2 Walk up and down your stairs, briskly, 20 times.

3 Grab two tins from the kitchen (baked beans will do!) and use them as dumbbells to give your forearms a workout.

PREPARING FOR THE FUTURE

Exercise (continued)

Today we are going to refresh your exercise plan, making sure that it's one that will last. Follow these tips and, remember, the single most important means of keeping going is to find a type of exercise that suits you.

♦ Write your sessions into your calendar or diary so that they become appointments you have to keep. If you're vague about them, it's easy to make an excuse to do something different.

♦ Begin an exercise journal. Write down how you feel after exercising. On the days when you don't feel like it, look back on the good workouts for some inspiration.

♦ See exercise as a treat. A simple shift in attitude can do wonders. Instead of seeing it as a chore, see exercise as something you're doing just for you, to make you feel better, to be kind to yourself and to boost your self-confidence.

♦ Set yourself goals. If you're going to the gym, ask the staff how you can record your progress. If brisk walking is more your style, a simple goal such as 'I will walk for half an hour, three times a week, for six weeks' is just as good a target.

♦ Keep reminding yourself that exercise can't fail to leave you feeling better – unless you overdo it that is!

♦ Don't think too big. If you think you have to exercise every day, you'll resent it. Give yourself two or three days off a week.

♦ It's always better to do some light exercise rather than nothing at all. If you usually go for a run, go for a walk if you feel tired. If you usually walk for half an hour, do 20 minutes on the days you'd rather stay inside.

♦ Vary your exercise. It can get boring if you do the same things all the time.

♦ Make the most of a good walk. Look around you – watch the seasons change as the year goes by.

♦ Before you exercise, think of coming home and doing something simple that you enjoy. It might be drinking a long glass of cold water, having a refreshing shower or cooking a healthy meal.

Activity

Think holistic!

- In this part of the programme you're bringing together the most important things you've learned under one roof. It's no good thinking, 'I feel confident, but I can't be bothered to exercise.' Everything must go together.

- Spend a few moments thinking of your mind and body as a whole. Imagine everything working in harmony.

- Everything complements everything else because you're taking care of every aspect of your mind and body.

Your commitment

Commit to making exercise a part of your new lifestyle. Build on those foundations by writing these words in your no-smoking notebook:

- I, ..., am a confident person.

- I eat a healthy diet.

- I enjoy exercising regularly.

- *Exercise – goal achieved.*

PREPARING FOR THE FUTURE

Interest and purpose

We all need to have something that motivates us in life, or we'd never get out of bed in the morning. This could be:

◆ your work
◆ your family
◆ your interests outside work and the family.

It doesn't matter what you like to do. Enjoying a quiet life is just as healthy a purpose as being a top sportsman or a successful business-woman.

> 'My life has no direction, no aim, no meaning and yet I'm
> happy. I can't figure it out. What am I doing right?'
> Charles M. Schulz, writer

But if anyone feels that their purpose in life is to smoke ... well, that's pretty sad! Thankfully if you're still with the 100-day programme now, you're out of that rut.

Be positive

If you don't have family, are unemployed or don't feel that you have any hobbies, you may have found it hard to complete the activity. But check that you're not thinking negatively. Rather than feeling bad about yourself, think about what you could do to improve things.

 TOP TIP

● How about volunteering in your local community? Check out the internet, local newspapers or your library for information.

Activity

What motivates you?

1 Under the headings, jot down whatever words come to mind to make three lists. Try to write at least three or four words in each column. An example for each is already given to get you started.

Work	Family	Interests
Busy	Kids	Friends

Remember to think about your life as a whole. For example, if you wrote 'boring' under the work column and you don't like your job at the moment, finding something that you enjoy doing in your free time will provide balance until you're in a position to look for a new job.

2 Now, think of some of the things you'd like to do in the future. Plan ahead – work out how you could make time for some new activities. Make some notes in your no-smoking book and follow these tips.

- Be realistic. If you have a new baby, you're unlikely to take up sky diving in the next few months!

- Keep it simple. Joining an art class, for example, is relatively inexpensive and will only take up one evening a week.

- Don't overdo it. You may have plenty of interests in your life already.

PREPARING FOR THE FUTURE

Keeping motivated

In the days after your Quit Day, we focused on some of the things you may have been missing about smoking. Gradually the sense of loss will lessen, but it's one of the reasons that former smokers relapse, even once the physical addiction is broken.

Maybe you still feel a sense of emptiness? That's why it's important to bring new things into your life.

⌖ TOP TIP

- Shore up your support network. People around you – especially those who've never smoked – will probably assume that you've completely forgotten about cigarettes by now. Let them know how valuable their encouragement has been throughout the programme – and remind them that words of encouragement are still important to you.

Activity

Are you over giving up?

Answer the following question.

If I feel an unexpected craving for a cigarette my first thought is:

a) I can't stand this craving, it's unbearable, I'll never get over not smoking.

b) Here we go again. I hate the feeling but I know it will be over soon.

c) I haven't had a craving for ages, so surely it would be OK to have a fag this time?

Answers

Answer a)

Although a craving is still an unpleasant experience for you, as long as you don't give in to it, you're still on the right track.

- Keep telling yourself that even though it's taking a long time, cravings will lessen in the months to come.

- Make sure you've done all you can to break the emotional link you have with smoking, by continuing to change the daily routines that remind you of cigarettes.

Answer b)

You seem to have everything under control.

- Use this result to reinforce your feelings of pride and self-confidence.

- Take care not to be complacent.

Answer c)

You're in dangerous territory.

- Keep thinking about your perceptions of smoking. If you still feel you're missing out, it's unlikely you'll stick with it long term.

- By having a cigarette you would not be 'treating' yourself. You would hate yourself for it, the moment you were down to the stub.

Techniques

Every day for 95 days, you have had a plan to follow and an activity to do. Even on the days where the activities have been quick to achieve, it has given you a structure that has consistently reinforced your decision not to smoke.

In five days' time you'll be on your own! It will be great to be a fully fledged non-smoker. But for the next couple of days we're going to make sure that you know what to do – automatically – if you find yourself in a situation that makes you want to smoke.

Why I gave up smoking

Successful quitters are the ones who began with clear reasons about why they wanted to stop. It's important that you never lose sight of those reasons, so write them in your notebook now.

You shouldn't need to think hard about these reasons. They should be constantly at the top of your mind so that you feel totally in control over your decision not to smoke.

No-smokers chart

- ◆ Make two columns on a piece of stiff card.
- ◆ Label the first 'Why I gave up' and the second 'Benefits of giving up'.
- ◆ Write your three reasons under each heading (see below).
- ◆ You need to see your non-smoker's chart every day.

Why I gave up	Benefits of giving up
◆ To feel in control.	◆ I am in control!
◆ For health reasons.	◆ I am fit and healthy!
◆ I hated the stigma.	◆ The stigma has gone!

Activity

You're on TV!

Today's task is to learn the reasons why you gave up smoking by heart.

- Imagine you're an actor learning their lines.

- Repeat the three reasons why you have given up smoking over and over again.

- Then get somebody to ask you: 'Why did you give up smoking?'

- Imagine you're being interviewed on television about your reasons.

- You would want to be confident, fluent and articulate about why you quit.

When your reasons for giving up smoking are embedded in your memory, do the same with the three main benefits of giving up smoking.

◆ You won't be looking in this book every day after NS+88, so think of your chart as a condensed reminder of the key points you have achieved.
◆ Prop it on a windowsill or pin it somewhere that will catch your eye.

This is an example of how your chart might look. But your reasons for giving up are personal – make sure you've thought them out for yourself!

PREPARING FOR THE FUTURE

Lifeskills

Today we're going to recap on all the practical activities and procedures that have contributed towards your success in giving up smoking. Although the programme specifically lasts for 100 days – these should last you forever. Long after cigarettes don't even feature in your daily thoughts, you can draw on these skills when life gets tough *for whatever reason*. The backbone of *Choker to Non-Smoker* has consisted of the following practical means of achieving a difficult task:

♦ visualisation
♦ positive thinking
♦ relaxation
♦ distraction.

Activity
Ways to support yourself

Copy the above list into your no-smoking notebook. Under each, write one example of how you've already implemented the technique. For example, '*Distraction*: always have a good book with me to read when my thoughts drift toward cigarettes.'

Skills for life

♦ Maybe you'll need to draw on them if you relapse and smoke a cigarette one day in the future.
♦ Maybe they'll be useful when the kids are being demanding.
♦ Maybe they'll get you through a tough time at work.

But once they're in place, your skills for life should define the capable way in which you deal with problem solving. Here are some new tips for each category:

Visualisation

◆ Picture how you want things to be, rather than how they are.
◆ Picture your body on the inside. How is it responding to what's going on?
◆ Picture a confident, assertive person dealing with a crisis. That person is you.

Positive thinking

◆ Change your everyday vocabulary.
◆ 'I can't' becomes 'I can'.
◆ Problems become *challenges*.
◆ Boredom become *opportunity*.

Relaxation

◆ Make an appointment with yourself to relax for one hour every week.
◆ Lock yourself in the bathroom and put a 'Do not disturb' sign on the door.
◆ Treat yourself to a massage.
◆ Give yourself some 'me time' to go for a stroll or have a coffee. (If you have a demanding family, do this alone. If you're short of company, book up a friend to share the time with in advance.)

Distraction

◆ Browse the magazine shelves in the newsagents. Choose one that you've never read before. Buy it! It may spark an interest.
◆ Plan a social event. Go to the theatre or cook for friends.
◆ Begin writing a novel or short story. If you finish it – great!

PREPARING FOR THE FUTURE

The rewards of not smoking are really beginning to kick in now.

♦ Your overall health is improving every day.
♦ Your heart, lungs and immune system are stronger.
♦ Your hair and skin is healthier.
♦ Your breath is fresh.
♦ You've saved loads of money!

Activity
Count your money

Set aside half an hour to tip your jar of cash out on the table and count it. Make a note of how much you've saved. Now you can decide how you'd like to spend it. Write down how much you have here:

£ ....

You could use it all up to celebrate finishing the 100-day programme, or you may prefer to keep the jar going for a few months and put it towards a big treat, such as a holiday.

Write down some ideas. You could ask the family which they think is best.

1 ....
2 ....
3 ....
4 ....
5 ....

How much nicer is this activity than the one where you filled up the jam jar with fag ends?!

TOP TIP

- Although we all have bills to pay, you deserve a reward for quitting smoking. Unless you're heavily in debt, use the money you've saved to treat yourself. Seeing a direct link between giving up the fags and being able to do or buy something special will mean more to you than using it for day-to-day necessities.

Quitter's quips

My wife and I gave up smoking at the same time. We kept the money jar going for six months after we stopped and saved about £1,500 between us. It was enough to afford a holiday in the sun. We went to Greece and had a wonderful time – staying in the nicest hotel we'd ever been in. It made us wish we'd given up years before, but better late than never! – Paul, 66

Top ten treats

There are plenty of ways to treat yourself with the money you've saved. Here are ten suggestions:

- Throw a celebration no-smokers' party.
- Book up a pampering day at a spa or health club.
- Go on holiday.
- Buy a new bike (it'll help your exercise regime).
- Check out the latest household gadgets – like a flat screen TV or a new computer.
- Pay an expert to makeover your garden.
- Take out gym membership.
- Buy a few cases of expensive wine.
- Spend a weekend break in a cosy hotel.
- Order fresh flowers for your home every week.

PREPARING FOR THE FUTURE

Remember that house you built to remind you of the strong foundations you have built as a non-smoker? Hopefully it's got a good kitchen, because today's task is to bake a cake.

First – take the ten-second test:

Quick quiz

Ten-second test

Within the last few days you've made commitments to stick with the five key points that will maximise your success as a non-smoker.

They are:

1 ....

2 ....

3 ....

4 ....

5 ....

Stop the watch! You should have been able to reel them off without thinking.

The answers are:

Self-esteem   Diet   Exercise   Interests   Lifeskills

You need to work on these five every day. But the small things in life also contribute significantly to a person's level of contentment.

TOP TIP

- Take yourself seriously. Lots of the activities in the 100-day programme have been fun to do. But not smoking is a serious business. If you let slip everything you've learned, you risk finding yourself having to start all over again. Visualise that thought for a few seconds!

Activity

Baking a cake

Imagine you are baking a cake. You have all the main ingredients, but to make it extra tasty, you are going to add a few extras. These are the simple things in life that make you happy – the icing on the cake, if you like. Research shows that the following things really make a difference to people's happiness (and they needn't cost a penny!):

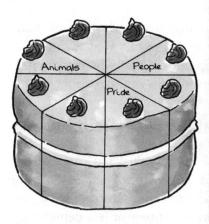

- giving and receiving attention to the people around you

- feeling emotionally connected with another living creature (human or a pet)

- feeling a sense of status. (This doesn't mean having a high-powered job. It just means doing things in life that you feel proud of.)

Think of some more. Imagine the cake can be sliced into pieces of eight. Three slices are taken – you need to fill in the rest.

After ten years of not smoking...

◆ Your risk of lung cancer falls to about half that of a smoker.

The final message that needs to sink in on your second-to-last day of the programme is this:

You – and only you – are responsible for yourself.

You may have had this book, help and support from friends and family as you've followed each day of the programme, but nobody could stop smoking for you. You did it. This also means that you are the only person who can make sure you don't start again.

Taking responsibility

Every individual has to take responsibility for their own emotional and physical wellbeing. Unfortunately nobody can wave a magic wand and make it easier for a person to cope in the world or make a person happier or less depressed. Once you learn to take responsibility for yourself, coping with all of life's ups and downs becomes easier. And keeping off the fags will be easier too. A new you is going to emerge when you turn over the final page of this book tomorrow.

Activity

The new you is here!

Choose the transformation that you like the best – and imagine how you're going to feel!

1   Caterpillar to butterfly.

2   Ugly duckling to beautiful swan.

3   Old banger to sleek sports car.

Or make up your own ...

....

'The past is another country.' L.P. Hartley, author

- You are now responsible for your own happiness.
- You can choose how you live your life.
- You can put your smoking past behind you.

Victim to survivor

Given that smoking is becoming increasingly unacceptable, it's likely that people who are unable or unwilling to stop will be seen as victims. This is already happening in America, where people who have developed lung cancer as a result of smoking, or heart disease through eating hamburgers, are taking legal action against the companies who sold them the products. The word 'victim' conjures up images of weakness, helplessness and lack of control. The word 'survivor' conjures up images of strength, determination and being in control. Which would you rather be?

Five thoughts to send you on your way

1 Use your fantastic achievement to spur you on to other achievements.
2 Take pride in being a non-smoker every day.
3 Accept yourself. You're unique and loveable for who you are.
4 Focus on your strengths and not your weaknesses.
5 Never smoke again. Just one cigarette could spark a downward spiral.

TOP TIP

- Remember you can't force other people to change – you can only be responsible for yourself. But if someone you love is still smoking, support them by telling them how good you feel and have a chat about today's programme so that they understand about taking responsibility.

After 15 years of not smoking...

- Your risk of a heart attack is the same as someone who has never smoked.

Congratulations! You've made it. You're a non-smoker

Today is a day for celebrating – you really do deserve it.

Don't let Day 100 – your 88th day as a non-smoker – slip by without marking the occasion. You needn't blow half the money you've saved, but you could:

♦ go out for dinner
♦ have friends round for a glass of champagne
♦ cook a nice meal for the family.

Activity

Bask in your success!

Today's only task is to bask in your success and take time out to think of what you've achieved and how you feel about yourself.

The test of time

People often ask, 'When can I truly relax?' They want to know when they can drop their guard and not have to steel themselves and think of their motivational techniques before they go out to a party or to the pub. It will take a while and time is the only true measure. After a year of not smoking (at all) it's unlikely you'll even think about cigarettes, even if people are smoking around you.

But here are a few scenarios that will help you gauge how you're doing.

♦ You're on holiday, sitting on the balcony of your hotel, watching the sunset. You have a glass of wine, but when someone offers you a cigarette, you say no and you mean no. *You are enjoying yourself more without one.*

- You're given some bad news. Maybe someone close to you has died or been diagnosed with a serious illness. Your first instinct is not to reach for a cigarette. *You will cope better without one.*

- You get roaring drunk on a stag night, hen night or at a family do. Everyone around you is urging you to have a fag for old times sake, or because 'one won't matter'. *You don't feel cornered. You are confident enough to hold your own.* Remember, as every day goes by from now onwards, you're getting stronger as a non-smoker and building a wider gap between the present and the past when you smoked.

Setting you up for success

You won't be reading this book every day now, but how about downloading this screensaver to keep you motivated over the next few weeks. It has:

- a calendar that shows how many days you've quit for
- a real-time day totaliser that counts the seconds you've stopped
- a selection of motivational statements to keep you on track
- a daily money calculator.

You can find it at the British Heart Foundation website: www.bhf.org.uk/smoking/swi_downloads.asp

---

(No more excuses!)

(14) **I smoked because I was addicted to the nicotine.**

You were addicted, physically and psychologically. But you're not any more.

You're free!

'Believe in yourself! Have faith in your abilities! Without a humble but reasonable confidence in your own powers you cannot be successful or happy.' Norman Vincent Peale, author, *The Power of Positive Thinking*

PREPARING FOR THE FUTURE

Your notes

USEFUL CONTACTS

The following organisations and charities all offer advice on giving up smoking.

Quit
The UK charity that helps people to give up smoking.
0800 00 22 00
www.quit.org.uk

NHS Smoking Helpline
0800 169 0 169
www.givingupsmoking.co.uk

Department of Health
www.dh.gov.uk

Patient UK
www.patient.co.uk

Cancer Research UK
www.cancerresearchuk.org

British Lung Foundation
www.lunguk.org

British Heart Foundation
www.bhf.org.uk

ASH (Action on Smoking and Health)
www.ash.org

BUPA
www.bupa.com

Net Doctor
www.netdoctor.co.uk